What people are saying about …

THE GRACE OUTPOURING

"Roy Godwin is going to rock you. This is the impressive story of one man, one couple, and their pleasure in following God—being obedient to his calling and his disciplines and bestowing his blessings. This book will likely change you … and perhaps even those around you."

Mark Batterson, lead pastor of National
Community Church in Washington,
DC, and author of the *New York Times*
best seller *The Circle Maker*

"*The Grace Outpouring* is the kind of book that changes your perspective on Jesus, his work, and the power he has to change lives, if only we'd believe him. It wooed me toward deeper, wider, live-out-loud prayer, and it beckoned me toward an adventurous life in the Spirit. I closed this book changed."

Mary DeMuth, author of *Everything: What You
Give and What You Gain to Become Like Jesus*

"Of the many books I've read in the past number of years, none has inspired, astonished, and convicted me like *The Grace Outpouring*. This book makes you hunger and thirst for God. The Celts used to speak of 'thin places,' where heaven brushes earth so closely you feel its breath, hear its whisper. Ffald-y-Brenin—*the Sheepfold of the King*—is such a place, and Roy Godwin's vivid account of it makes you want to board a plane tonight and get there by morning. But one thing surpasses visiting a thin place: becoming one yourself. Read the book, and so begin."

Mark Buchanan, author of
Your Church Is Too Safe

"Get ready to have your passion for prayer stirred like never before!"

Shannon Ethridge, MA, author and advocate
for healthy sexuality and spirituality

the
GRACE
OUTPOURING

the
GRACE
OUTPOURING

Becoming a People of Blessing

ROY GODWIN & DAVE ROBERTS

David C Cook®
transforming lives together

THE GRACE OUTPOURING
Published by David C Cook
4050 Lee Vance Drive
Colorado Springs, CO 80918 U.S.A.

David C Cook U.K., Kingsway Communications
Eastbourne, East Sussex BN23 6NT, England

The graphic circle C logo is a registered trademark of David C Cook.

The website addresses recommended throughout this book are offered as a resource to you. These websites are not intended in any way to be or imply an endorsement on the part of David C Cook, nor do we vouch for their content.

Unless otherwise noted, all Scripture quotations are taken from the Holy Bible, New International Version®, NIV®. Copyright © 1973, 1984 by Biblica, Inc.™ Used by permission of Zondervan. All rights reserved worldwide. www.zondervan.com. Scripture quotations marked ESV are taken from The Holy Bible, English Standard Version® (ESV®), copyright © 2001 by Crossway, a publishing ministry of Good News Publishers. Used by permission. All rights reserved; and KJV are taken from the King James Version of the Bible.

The author has changed some names in this book to protect privacy.

LCCN 2012943546
ISBN 978-0-7814-0846-2
eISBN 978-1-4347-0416-0

The Team: Terry Behimer, Amy Konyndyk, Jack Campbell, Karen Athen
Cover Design: Nick Lee
Cover Photo: Shutterstock

Printed in the United States of America
Second Edition 2012

8 9 10 11 12 13 14 15 16 17

011717

DEDICATION

Roy Godwin

*To Daphne, our wonderful family, the team, and
all those connected with God's work here. You
inspire and bless me. Let's go and explore further.*

Dave Roberts

*To all the people at Living Stones,
Eastbourne. Let's persevere together.*

FFALD-Y-BRENIN
pronounced **Fal** (as in *pal*) **duh brennin**
meaning "The Sheepfold of the King"

God is too great to need our exaggeration. This book contains many testimonies as spoken to us by guests at various times. We want to be as accurate as possible. If the reader is aware of any error, please let us know, so that we may correct it in any future editions.

CONTENTS

FOREWORD

You're about to read a story. It's a tale of a quite unexpected spiritual unfolding on a Welsh hillside far from the media strategies, church-growth seminars, and everyday programs of conventional church life. In keeping with God's pattern of using marginal people from obscure places—I'm thinking fishermen, tax collectors, children, women, and Galileans during Jesus' time on earth—this story sees God intrude into the mundane rhythms of life in a Christian retreat center, run by a couple who would have been forgiven for opting for a quiet life when they arrived in this quiet Welsh valley.

The narrator of this story will be Roy, but before you become immersed in the story, I want to let you know why we're telling it. As his coauthor, I would like to commend Roy to you and tell you a little of how we wrote it.

Roy has a vision to see houses of prayer established throughout Britain and Europe, and particularly throughout the Mediterranean nations. This has grown out of the reality of what has happened at Ffald-y-Brenin, as the community there has committed to a rhythm of prayer, thankfulness, and blessing. One's natural instinct when a vision is crowding itself into every available space in your imagination is to write it down, surround the ideas with biblical references, and urge all within earshot to take heed.

But as people who model our lives on a storyteller, we're best advised to do as he did and tell the stories of what God has done. So we invite you to join us as this story unfolds. We'll draw out principles and go to the root sources in Scripture, but we hope that what you read will help paint pictures on the canvas of your imagination that will allow you to be provoked by the Holy Spirit to prayer, compassion, and a mind-set that desires to bless others.

Roy is a short, bearded, hospitable man. He's patient with people but has an evangelist's hunger to see lives transformed by the life and message of Jesus. He is gentle, but there's also a certain steeliness, a tough-minded realism that holds people accountable and doesn't flinch from the helpful but often difficult question. There is a persistent humility about him too, demonstrated as he leaves people to hear from God after praying for them. Their subsequent encounters with the Holy Spirit are clearly God's work, as Roy has usually quietly excused himself from the scene.

The story you're about to read was told to me by Roy over four autumn days. We talked together in the room where the late Rob Lacey brought much of the Scripture to life with his acclaimed *Street Bible*. We sat in the ancient but warm cottage and talked, our conversation rising and falling with gentle rhythms not unlike the bubbling stream that ran outside the window. But on occasion the tempo quickened as the sense of what the Holy Spirit was doing there on the hillside caused a rush of facts, emotion, and wonder to break like a rain-swollen river around our ears.

So these are Roy's words, crafted by me and expanded by both of us. We're praying that this story travels around the world much as the *Street Bible* did and provokes houses of prayer wherever it is read.

Be blessed.

Dave Roberts
www.tahilla.com

Dave is a former editor of both *Renewal* and *Christianity* magazines and the coauthor of *Red Moon Rising*—the story of 24–7 Prayer.

CHAPTER 1

WE BLESS YOU IN THE NAME OF JESUS

I was desperate. Despite a series of miracles that had enabled my wife, Daphne, and me to become directors of a beautiful Welsh Christian retreat center, I was frightened that I had made a mistake. As I thought about it, I realized that for the first time in maybe thirty-five years, several months had passed during which I hadn't clearly brought somebody to the knowledge of Jesus. I believed I had a calling on my life to bring people to Jesus, so what was happening?

I wasn't to know it, but God was hours away from showing me some unexpected answers. In the meantime the frustration mounted. It had been partly provoked by my visit to a business conference in Pembroke in the west of Wales. I had spent the day with two hundred businessmen and women. I felt at home among them. This was the type of pool I had fished in for most of my life.

As I reflected on my suit-clad outing to the hotel on the estuary, the agitation grew. Instead of being with the Christians who came to the center to recharge and reflect, I needed to be with those who had no clear Christian understanding and commitment. I decided the only thing I could do was leave the center.

The next morning I sat in our farmhouse-style kitchen and poured out, with some passion, the details of my agitated day with the businessmen to my ever-patient wife: "It's just no good. I cannot stay here any longer. I need to immerse myself in the everyday lives of people without a Christian faith so I can just be me and share my faith with them."

Daphne, petite and blonde, is always full of incredible wisdom and insight, and she just calmly looked at me and said, "Hmm. Well, if that's how you feel, and you feel so strongly, it's about time you told God about it."

Suitably rebuked, I retreated to the upstairs office to pray. Fortunately I wasn't aware that her internal response was actually *Well, you can leave if you like, but I'm not!* That just might have affected my conversation with God, which was going something like "Lord, I need to be spending time with people who don't know you. I cannot survive unless I'm doing this, because this is what you made me to be, this is what I am … somebody who introduces people to you, who connects them, or fans the flame." The pent-up emotions surfaced in my jumbled words. "How can I be whom you created me to be unless I am sharing you with those who don't know you, or seeking to heal the hurting, or fanning flames of passion in those who are on the fringes of walking with you? What am I without you? How can I live unless I obey your call? How can I be someone else? Lord, something has got to happen. I cannot stay here unless you do something."

My talk with God finished, I returned to the everyday rhythms of life at Ffald-y-Brenin. Within hours there was a knock at the door. Tall and middle-aged, the couple calling on us were strangers.

"Hello, I hope you don't mind us calling like this, but I wonder if you could tell us what this place is."

We sat them down at our table, where we had just finished lunch, and the reason for their trek up our long and steep drive unfolded.

"Well, we were driving along here, and we don't quite understand it, but we were compelled to come up your drive." They had noted that it was a Christian retreat center, but that meant little to them. We made them a cup of tea, always a good place to start, and then talked in general terms about the center for a while before finally explaining to them that this is a place where lives get changed because God is real.

They liked the idea of being shown around, so we guided them through the garden, with its special rockery, swiftly flowing stream, and a beautiful view of the valley and surrounding hills. We took in the stone corridors of the main retreat center, walked around the grounds, and back to the final room, which happened to be the chapel. There they seemed to sense something of the presence of God, although they might not have been able to articulate what was happening to them. They sat down rather speedily, rather heavily, as though their legs had gone a little weak.

I immediately created a new tradition: "We have a rule here about how we respond to our visitors. We like to bless them before they leave. May I bless you?"

They had no problem with that, so I simply said, "I bless you in the name of Jesus to know God, his purpose for your life, and his blessings on you and your family and the situations of your life. Amen."

They started to weep. The sense of the presence of God seemed tangible. I quietly let myself out of the chapel so they wouldn't be embarrassed by my presence. It was time to let God do what he wanted to do for that couple.

A little later they came and found me, full of gratitude and rather shaken by what was for them the unexpected sense of God's presence. I was able to share a little more of the good news of Jesus before they left.

Being a somewhat strange, fallible creature, I didn't connect their visit with my earlier prayer. So God sent someone else to my door to help me connect the spiritual dots. The next day another knock on the door was followed by the same inquiring words:

"Hello, could you tell us what this place is and what goes on here?" At last, as I went through the social pleasantries, it was dawning on me: this was God's response to my prayer. That became clearer the more we talked. They had no Christian faith and didn't seem very interested in God. They had sensed something and were simply curious.

While we may like to think that spiritual breakthrough will be surrounded by stirring worship and heartfelt preaching, we now began to observe a pattern that involved the simple hospitality of welcome, cups of tea, scenic tours and moments, and then a few minutes—or sometimes hours—of profound encounter with the Holy Spirit.

Our latest couple was open to the idea of a prayer of blessing when they reached the chapel, so I mentioned our tradition.

This time the Holy Spirit came with even more manifest power, and they wept profusely. But still it seemed right to slip away and leave them to hear from God.

Later, as we prayed together with our ever-changing community, we said to God, "Lord, we like what you're doing, and we bless what you're doing. Lord, would you please do more of it?" And he did. For a period of time, each day, we would pray and say, "Lord, would you please send someone else?" And he would. Many people came up the drive. (In fact, God started sending so many people that today there is a reception area for them where they are greeted by team members.)

It wasn't always straightforward. One afternoon I was interrupted by a knock at the door, and there stood another inquiring couple. Faced with a deadline for posting a form, I was internally wavering; but our hospitality habit prevailed and the kettle went on for tea. We did the tour and got to the chapel, but even before I could pray the prayer of blessing, they were visibly touched by the Holy Spirit. I slipped away to post my form. Later I was able to talk with them and explain what God had been doing.

As they walked away to their car, another couple walked toward me. *No! I've got to get this work finished,* I thought, even as I outwardly smiled. *Lord, I haven't got time for this now; please turn the flow off!*

I explained to the couple that I was a little pressed but asked how I could help. I wasn't anticipating the man's response: "I was driving along, going through the valley, enjoying this beautiful summer afternoon, and the weirdest thing happened when I got to your drive. I've held my driving license for over forty years, but I was compelled to come up your drive, and I'm absolutely convinced that if I'd taken my hands off the wheel, it would've just turned and the car would've found its way up here. I don't understand it. I've never experienced anything like it. Could you please tell us what on earth's going on here?"

I explained that we were a Christian retreat center, a place where the presence of God comes and people's lives are changed because they encounter him.

"How interesting," he said. "That reminds me of the story of the bishop and the prostitute."

By now we were at the kitchen table, and he was telling a pornographic story while his wife blushed with embarrassment.

I was finding all of this very difficult, but nevertheless I offered them a cup of tea. To my intense disappointment they said yes. While the kettle was boiling, he told another story that was even worse than the first one.

I was ready to do some righteous rebuking. I didn't want this in Ffald-y-Brenin, in my house and in my kitchen; but God said to me, "Don't you dare rebuke this man." It was that clear. This worried me. It was not the prompting I wanted to hear. I wondered whether it was God's voice that I was discerning after all.

We heard a third filthy story, and I explained more about the center and what we believed about the presence of God there. When he started his fourth story, I just wanted to be rid of them. But I had made a commitment to God in the previous weeks that if he brought people to the center I would stop, however pressed I was, put them first, and bless them. So I offered to show them around, hoping they would take the chance to make their escape and save me time and irritation. But his wife said yes, and the object of my wrath mumbled something about tagging along though not really being interested. I resisted the temptation to suggest he wait in the car.

The center was packed with guests, so I walked them around via the outside paths. However, we had to pass windows thrown open because of the heat of the day, and the stream of profane anecdotes did not slow down. Internally I was having an animated conversation with God: *Please protect the hearing of the guests as this filth is paraded past their windows. Lord, I am committed to blessing this couple, but this is a real struggle.*

When we reached the chapel, I told them what the building was, then opened the door and ushered them in. The husband was in full obscene flow. Then he put one step on the stone floor of the chapel, fell headlong to the ground, and began to cry like a baby. He cried out to God, "I'm so sorry. I didn't know you were real. I've heard so much about you and not really believed, and not cared, but I didn't know you were real. Oh God, I'm so dirty. Oh God, how can you ever cleanse me? Oh God, can you ever have mercy on me?"

His wife's legs had given way too, and she'd fallen very heavily onto the stone seating. She sat and wept. I quietly slipped out and let God do his work.

This slipping away was an important part of our ethos. I wanted people to have direct dealings with God. When visitors left, we didn't want them to feel that there was somebody at Ffald-y-Brenin who had led them and taught them, to whom they must speak when they had difficulties in the future. I wanted people to know that God himself had come and met with them, that he was able to convict and counsel them, and that they could speak to him directly—they didn't need to be taught "special words" to pray. If I had been present through these encounters, they might have asked how to pray or been scared to admit that they didn't know how to pray. Afterward, when people would tell us their stories of wonder and weeping, we would explain and encourage, offering them a context for what had happened and suggesting how to find out more about God the Father, Jesus, and the Holy Spirit.

Several patterns began to emerge in the months that followed. We often did not need to offer to pray a prayer of blessing, as the Holy Spirit fell on people spontaneously as they walked around the center or the grounds. Our job was to go along with what the Holy Spirit was doing and to continue to bless what he was doing and respond to it.

It was so rewarding to speak blessings on the people God brought along who didn't know him, so we turned our sights outward and began a pattern of speaking blessings into the local community. Every Friday morning in our chapel meeting we would speak blessings over the neighborhood. The valley below us has a two-mile section that you could call our locality. It is home to about eighty people scattered across its half-mile width.

Gradually a structure emerged as we continued in our new tradition of blessing prayer, and we now pray in that pattern as a matter of course. We pray for people and we pray for households. We speak into every household, blessing it in the name of Jesus. We're not interceding; we're speaking to them in the name of Jesus.

The phrase "We bless you from Zion" captures a biblical attitude to prayer that we wanted to apply to our context when we used the words "We bless you from Ffald-y-Brenin, this place where God's presence is being poured out. We speak to you in his name, and we bless you."

So we bless every household, we bless every marriage, we bless the relationship between family members of different generations, and we bless their health and their wealth. We bless the work of their hands. We bless every wholesome enterprise they're involved with, that they may prosper.

Because we're in an agricultural community, we bless the flocks and the herds, and we bless the grass so that it will be nutritious in winter—which it wouldn't normally be—and will not need to be supplemented in order to strengthen the animals.

We bless supportive networks of friendship that run through the community, because they're a sign of the kingdom. We bless the pupils of our rural school and ask God to aid their learning. We bless the teachers and pray that school may be a safe and wholesome place, where simple childlike trust and belief in God and in Jesus can be comfortably maintained.

We pray for both places of worship in the valley, that the word of God and the Spirit of God may flow out from both.

Then we speak to the hearts of all the people who are in the community. We bless them to be safe and to be softened, so they may become more and more responsive to the voice of God. We bless them with the overspill of the kingdom of heaven being made manifest here in Ffald-y-Brenin.

Before long we began to see the fruit of these prayers in quite miraculous ways. A man who rented a small stable in the community and did agricultural repairs had not been finding things easy. After we began blessing the valley in the name of Jesus, his business suddenly began to take off. He had to acquire larger premises and employ people and was able to buy his own house.

The lambing season came, and more miracles emerged. We had been blessing the ewes to be strong and healthy and productive. One of our farmer neighbors told us how he'd been absolutely stunned by the number of quads and triplets being born to his ewes. His normal hope was for many twins. The ewes were coping well, but his wife was run off her feet supporting the rest of the lambs with bottle feeds!

He wasn't the only farmer with a story to tell. Another one stopped me in the road and said, "Come and look in this field with me." Just beyond the gate was a massive bull. He carefully walked around the bull with an arm stiffened in front of him as if to ward off an attack. The bull was staring at him and slowly turning and facing him as he walked around. The farmer invited me to join him. I declined. He insisted. I closed the gate and refused again. Now he was stuck in the field with the bull and had an obstinate onlooker.

He managed to divide off a cow and her calf and invited me to consider how excellent the calf's rear end was. Being no expert on bovine hindquarters, I merely murmured some niceties. He had to spell it out for me. The calf was clearly, given the breadth of its rear, going to be a superb bull. It seems that farmers pray that at least once in a lifetime they will have a calf like that one.

He still clearly felt I wasn't grasping how good this was. "I had one like this last year as well. It's completely unnatural." I told him that we had been praying that the blessings of God would fall on the cattle, on the herds of the locality. Another seed was planted in another life as God's blessing unfolded in the life of a farmer in this green valley in Pembrokeshire.

But there was more. A lady who lives out in the wilds at the head of the valley runs a farmhouse bed and breakfast. Suddenly she was awarded AA landlady of the year for Great Britain and was busy at awards, on publicity trips, and in TV studios. Even now we tease her and tell her we're having a plaque put up at Ffald-y-Brenin, which will claim we are friends of the award-winning Lilwen MacAllister.

This remote valley was seeing material and spiritual blessing. The chapel had not had a baptism for a good few years, but after we prayed the prayer of blessing, a dam seemed to break. One very cold day, muddy underfoot, we were able to witness about seven people being baptized in the open-air baptistery, fed by the local stream.

My old ways of sharing my faith were being changed as this understanding of blessing people began to not merely take hold of our hearts but actually bear fruit in our community.

I was no stranger to the "truth and Scripture" method. This appeal to the mind is valid, good, and powerful for many. But for people who don't consider themselves particularly literate and for those who have moved to a more visual, "discovered in life" knowledge, it can often fail to stir their hearts, minds, and emotions.

I had started to challenge the "faith as normal" mind-set that I felt many Christians had slipped into. I had already begun to question a culture of faith that places a high value on correcting strangers. For example, we're very good at throwing stones at politicians and the media. Christians seem very keen on petitions. I started to ask people who wanted to publicize their petition objecting to a particular broadcast, for instance, whether they had ever previously commended the broadcaster for programs that were wholesome. Were they praying for the media or was this simply mudslinging?

Having a heart to bless will challenge the judgmental mind-set that can color how we look at those we live with and among. We can become a "grace first" people. We're still asking people to turn away from rebellion against God, but we're seeking to be part of the revelation from the Father that his primary desire is to bless those he created in his image.

If we will let the wisdom of God inhabit our thinking, a consistent "grace first" pattern will emerge in our actions and words. "Grace first" prayer for healing doesn't search for wrongdoing in a person's life that needs correcting as a prelude to a miracle. There doesn't seem to be much evidence for that approach in the ministry of Jesus. We simply ask that the power of God should touch that life.

As goodness, grace, and mercy are manifest, we can remind people to change their ways—they're ready to hear the words of correction when they've heard the shout of love. Jesus, for instance, saved a sinful adulterous woman from death and then gently suggested that she "go and sin no more."

Think for a moment about your experience with God. Sometimes a truth enters your life and you value it. It becomes a thread in your tapestry of faith. Then a season comes when you realize how important that insight is. The idea of blessing people, already growing in our lives, took hold of me in a new way as our life at Ffald-y-Brenin unfolded, despite the attacks that it also released.

We found that there is often resistance to heart habits that incline toward grace. There were plenty of Christians who told me that our practice of blessing people who were not yet Christian was absolutely wrong. We were advised that it would be much better to cry out to God to make things much worse for them. Such people were not pleased to be told that this type of prayer was like a curse.

I cannot find a home in faith houses built on judgment. My personal experience is that God has had favor on me and shown me mercy when I don't deserve it. I have been disobedient and apathetic, but the mercy that he's poured out on me has taken my breath away. When we hear the testimonies of wretched sinners who have found salvation, we rejoice with them and the angels.

The lower they have been, the greater the glory. It is not quite as straightforward when it is someone who is already a Christian, whose life has imploded, and that had been my experience. I know that if I were God I wouldn't have given someone like me another chance.

As these understandings had taken hold in my life in the years prior to coming to Ffald-y-Brenin, I concluded I didn't want to persuade people about the veracity or nonveracity of the words in a book. I believed they could encounter the living God and that the words would come alive to them as a result.

Asking people if we can bless them is an offer that few refuse. We're not saying, "Can we pray for you in a general way?" We're not putting a difficult burden on those doing the praying. Blessing someone is simple and easy. The Holy Spirit comes because, when you bless, you are reflecting something that the Father is doing and speaking words that the Father desires to be said.

God's desire to bless is absolutely outrageous. Nothing can stop him. He has set himself with immovable intent to bless mankind. His longing is that Jesus shall have many brothers and sisters. That's us. Before we knew him, he knew us. Before we loved him, he loved us. He designed us for a purpose wrapped up in blessing. Heaven, our ultimate destination, is full of blessing, and we are invited to pray for the coming of heaven on earth right now.

When the practice of priesthood was originally about to commence, God instructed Moses to explain to Aaron how he and the priests were to act. Not only were they to intercede for the people but they were to pronounce blessings over them as well. "The LORD spoke to Moses, saying, 'Speak to Aaron and his sons, saying, Thus you shall bless the people of Israel: you shall say to them, The LORD bless you and keep you; the LORD make his face to shine upon you and be gracious to you; the LORD lift up his countenance upon you and give you peace'" (Numbers 6:22–26 ESV).

Then came a remarkable explanation and insight: "So shall they put my name upon the people of Israel, and I will bless them" (v. 27). God placed into the mouths of the priests the power to speak words that caused God to unleash transformational, life-changing blessings upon the people. This is in line with our understanding that when people on earth are in agreement with the word from heaven, the power of the age to come is released in the here and now on earth.

We make a great mistake if we believe that this is simply wordy theology. "Then Aaron lifted up his hands toward the people and blessed them, and he came down from offering the sin offering and the burnt offering and the peace offerings" (Leviticus 9:22 ESV). Sounds rather formal and religious, doesn't it? Yet God's kingdom does not consist of words but of power.

So notice what happened next in verses 23–24: "And Moses and Aaron went into the tent of meeting, and when they came out they blessed the people, and the glory of the LORD appeared to all the people. And fire came out from before the LORD and consumed the burnt offering and the pieces of fat on the altar, and when all the people saw it, they shouted and fell on their faces." What a difference is made to the priesthood when the blessing comes from an encounter, a meeting with God himself! The supernatural is released, the glory of God is seen, and praise arises to him.

You might think, as Aaron probably did, that speaking out blessings is an easy enough thing to do, but most people find that it is quite difficult to learn. Invariably they start to intercede, asking the Father to bless. Although that is a very good thing to do, it is then prayer, not the speaking out of blessing. Speaking or pronouncing blessings does not replace prayer and intercession but is a companion to them, and they should be regularly found together.

When we bless, we look the person in the eye (if that is the situation) and speak directly to him or her. For instance, we may say something like "I bless you in the name of the Lord that the grace of the Lord Jesus might rest upon you. I bless you in his name that the Father's love might surround you and fill you, that you may know in your deepest being just how fully and completely he accepts you and rejoices over you."

Notice the personal pronoun *I*. It is *I* who is pronouncing blessing in the name of Jesus over the person directly. I have not prayed to God for a blessing but have spoken a blessing using the authority Jesus gives us to pronounce blessing on the people so that he may come and bless them. This is what Jesus commissioned us to do when he drew us into the Kingdom of Priests!

But what exactly should we bless people with? What should we say? First we ask the Holy Spirit to help us with the words to bless before we begin, so that the people receive the blessing that the Father wishes to pour out on them; his insight, not ours; his words, not ours.

We want to bless the whole person, and many people find that the well-used blessings acronym helps them be creative in blessing.

B   Body: health, protection, strength

L   Labor: work, income, security

E   Emotional: joy, peace, hope

S   Social: love, marriage, family, friends

S   Spiritual: salvation, faith, grace

So, for instance, we may bless someone as follows, using the blessings acronym as a help: "I bless you in the name of Jesus that the fullness of his peace may flood your heart and mind, sinking deeply into every part of your being and life. I bless you that your body may be strengthened and healed so that you are free to walk in the joy of the Lord."

We need to be clear at all times that we are blessing in the name of Jesus with his authority and anointing. All power and authority resides in him, including the power and authority to bless.

Blessings can be spoken over people, whether present or absent; homes; towns, areas, regions, nations; land, businesses, livestock, schools, etc.

In Deuteronomy 10:8 (ESV, reinforced in 21:5) we read: "At that time the LORD set apart the tribe of Levi to carry the ark of the covenant of the LORD to stand before the LORD to minister to him and to bless in his name, to this day." Wow! What a ministry: to carry the presence, to minister to the Lord, and to speak blessings in his name to the people!

Now here is a wonderful truth. When Jesus came, he was revealed as our High Priest. He is the presence, filled without measure, ministering to God and releasing incredible blessings upon all who can receive, including us. Yet there is more. You and I are now called into a new priesthood, that of all believers. We are to carry the presence, minister to God, and speak, pronounce, invoke, release blessings upon people. "But you are a chosen race, a royal priesthood, a holy nation, a people for his own possession, that you may proclaim the excellencies of him who called you out of darkness into his marvelous light" (1 Peter 2:9 ESV).

There is a significant hymn by Charles Wesley that says, "My God, I know, I feel thee mine." There is an important balance in those words. We need to know God at the level of our minds and our understanding, but we also need to experience him. The Bible encourages us to taste and see that he is good. If we can bless people, and the Holy Spirit comes and overshadows them and breaks them, they are eager to know who this God is that they've tasted. It's wonderful. If God wants to move with people like that as a response to blessing, I want to play a part in it.

And as these first inklings stirred in us—thoughts of what the practice of blessing people might bring—we were not to know just how profound a challenge would come to "faith as usual" from this gentle but insistent work of the Holy Spirit.

Chapter 2

ARE YOU AN ANGEL?

I am not normally the one who answers the bookings line, but on this occasion I did, and it was to be an intriguing conversation. The caller was a university tutor wanting to bring her class of mature students to Ffald-y-Brenin for an afternoon. She was keen to know if I would be there, which seemed a little odd. She seemed unconcerned about when the center was free or what size rooms we had. Puzzled, I asked her why they were coming. Was it for a study afternoon? "No," she said. "Somebody told me that if I bring people to Ffald-y-Brenin, you will bless them." I asked if they were a Christian group. She said they were not.

The group came one sunny afternoon and listened carefully as we served them tea and scones with jam and cream and told them a little bit about the history of Ffald-y-Brenin, as well as gently sharing a few of our more recent stories. As was our practice, we offered them a tour, and when they were all seated in the chapel, I double-checked that they were happy to be blessed. "If anybody's uncomfortable with it, then the door is just here. I've left it open, so please slip out and we'll just be a few moments." They were vociferous: "No, it's what we've come for." And so I had the joy of blessing them.

From this small beginning more opportunities arose. An adult learning group visited the chapel, and we had the privilege of asking God to bless their ability to learn, to bless their learning skills, but also to bless them to be able to know everything that God wanted them to learn, so that they could be the people he really planned for them to be.

We find that some people weep and some are quite broken as the presence of God comes. So, what is happening to them?

We've already noted that "putting the name of God" upon people when we bless them is referenced in Numbers 6:27. We're invoking the very character of God himself into the lives of those we pray for. They're getting a foretaste of being adopted into God's family. We're opening a door for them to glimpse something of the kingdom of God. God is saying, "I'm going to bless you with everything I've blessed my children with." We're releasing the blessings of Abraham upon them. We have simply enabled God to do something within the constraints that he has placed on the way he works, so that blessing comes on these people. This is another illustration of God's way of treating us. The measure we use toward others will be the measure that he uses toward us. As we forgive we will be forgiven (Matthew 6:14–15). As we bless we will be blessed (Genesis 12:3).

In Luke 10, the disciples were instructed to declare the peace of God over the towns they entered. For us today, that means asking God to manifest his character in the communities we live in. As we pray using the revealed names of God, he will come and show his beauty, mercy, and compassion.

I've come to believe that God exists to bless. It is an impulse that is at the heart of his character. In the community of the Trinity, the proto-community that is our supreme example, the blessing flows between Father, Son, and Holy Spirit. The Father loves and blesses the Son, and the Son loves and blesses the Father, and the Holy Spirit loves and blesses both, and they love and bless him.

In that relationship we see the unstoppable flow of love and mercy that is God. I once had a picture, a visual image in my imagination, that caused me to view him as a greyhound at the starting block, simply waiting for the word, for the gate to be lifted, and he's off. God is slow to anger and swift to bless, and he desires to bless both the righteous and the unrighteous alike. Somehow we release something here on earth when we're acting in unison with the cry of heaven. The kingdom is released when there's an agreement between heaven and earth. His will can be done on earth, just as it is in heaven.

As the adult learning group members were leaving, I walked to the minibus with them. The leader turned to me and said, "If only my husband had been here." Her husband was bedridden, the prognosis wasn't good, and his exhausted wife was both working and caring for him. I suggested we bless him in his absence anyway. She was a bit surprised, but in a few moments we began to pray, in the inauspicious context of the car park, asking God to bless her husband in the name of Jesus and to release further blessing into his life.

The next day I got a call. After dropping the students off, she had driven home. As she parked her car, her fully dressed husband ran out of the house, wrapped his arms around her, and said, "I've prepared a meal for you." He told her that at five o'clock something very strange had come over him and he knew that he was now okay. She in turn knew that was exactly the time that we'd blessed him.

It wasn't long before another visitor disrupted our previous way of thinking and ushered in another chapter in the work of the Holy Spirit among us. An American-sounding woman called and asked if she could come and stay. She wanted to come that day and stay for a week, but she had no money. I sensed God was at work in the situation and told her that her lack of money needn't be a barrier. She didn't sound too thrilled, which I found a little puzzling.

It then transpired that she didn't have any transportation from the nearest town, so Daphne went to pick up what I assumed was a woman in her fifties, but she returned with a raised eyebrow signaling that our assumptions had been wrong.

Our visitor was a young woman in her midtwenties, attractive, swarthy, and smelling not a little of patchouli or maybe even cannabis. We sat her down at the table, and she explained that she was a new age traveler, but she'd come to a point where she just needed to get away from her live-in boyfriend and everybody else and make a little bit of sense of her life. She had tried to book in at some new age retreats and a Buddhist center that wanted her to spend some months purifying herself, because she was a woman, before they would let her in. She had become desperate and thought maybe she should check out our Christian center—all the while hoping we would say no. Our positive responses had left her with mixed emotions.

Daphne and I had a brief whisper together and offered her a place if she would help us for an hour a day. (We invented a cleaning job because we wanted her to feel that she was contributing toward her keep.) We were going to put her in a small spare room, but Daphne felt we should give her the best we had. We showed her the room and gave her a note about our chapel times. We told her she would be very welcome but that there was no pressure to attend.

The next morning she came to chapel and was part of our morning worship cycle: a song, a prayer, a reflective reading of a psalm, a time of silence, reflective prayer out of that reading, and a final prayer. She thought we had just celebrated Mass! It was clear that she had little knowledge of everyday Christianity. So I gave her a sheet based on a reflection after each meal of the day. There was a brief Bible reading for each meal and a one-line prayer that simply said, "Lord, if your word is true, reveal it to me. Amen." I also gave her a Bible, a notepad, and a pen and encouraged her to write down notes, her questions, and anything she thought was coming to her from the Scriptures. I made it clear that we wouldn't check whether she had done it and we didn't need to see what she had written.

On Friday we sat down after morning chapel for a coffee. She started to explain to me why she disliked Christians. (Mmm … this wasn't what I was expecting to hear after all our free hospitality!) She objected to the claim made by Christians that Jesus is the only way to God. In her mind it was obvious that there were hundreds of different ways to God, and to claim otherwise was arrogant. I explained that the opinion of Christians was not the key issue. What was more crucial was what Jesus had said. He claimed to be "the way and the truth and the life" and was clear that nobody could come to the Father except through him (John 14:6). I gently suggested that here was the crunch issue. Would she respond to Christ's words?

She wanted to debate this, but I told her it was time for her to go and carry on with her plans for the rest of the day. She was taken aback. I told her I was not prepared to debate Jesus' words. If she had an issue with those words, she needed to talk to Jesus about them. In the end I had to put my hand on her back and gently steer her out of the door because she didn't want to go. She wanted to debate it.

The next day was Saturday, and Daphne and I were savoring the thought of getting up late and generally lazing around. But it wasn't to be. Early in the day there was a hammering on our door. We shuffled downstairs, pulling our dressing gowns on, and opened the door to our American guest. She was trembling, shaking with excitement.

"Why haven't you told me the truth? Why have you not told me the truth?" she repeated.

I said, "I'm sorry. What do you mean?"

She said, "Why didn't you tell me that God is my Father, that he made me, that he has a plan for my life? Why didn't you tell me that he loves me desperately, that I've never been on my own? Why didn't you tell me this? Why didn't you tell me that Jesus really is his Son, that when he died he took my sin? Why didn't you tell me that God raised him to life? Why didn't you tell me that he's exalted him to his right hand? Why didn't you tell me that Jesus can come now into my heart to live and make me a new person? Why didn't you tell me this?"

I stood there, open mouthed, and asked, "How do you know all this?"

"Because he's done it this morning, hasn't he? He's come into my heart and he's changed me; I'm a new person. Why didn't you tell me all this?"

I thought perhaps the conversation should carry on in the kitchen. She came in, barely drew breath, and plunged on. "I'm just so excited that he's come. I didn't know that he was like this. Why didn't you tell me?" It transpired that she had been doing the readings and praying the prayer every mealtime.

Then she looked at me and said, "You didn't tell me about the fire." I wasn't sure what to think given what she had told us about her new age background and drug experimentation. "You didn't tell me that God has fire, and he can put his fire on you so that you can blaze for him, and when you encounter other people, the fire he's put on you can touch other people, so they catch fire for him as well."

So far, so good. It wasn't quite the way I'd express it, but her words had truth at their heart. A simple encounter with God had sparked this in her, and she was speaking it out as she had come to understand it.

Daphne and I had to go out later, but when we returned at teatime, she rushed to see us, full of fresh news. "I'm afraid things have been going on in your absence, and I don't know if it's okay." Again I trembled inwardly, but once more my concern about spiritual confusion melted away as her story unfolded.

She had decided to walk into our nearest little town, Newport, a four-mile hike. On her way she saw a man walking toward her. As she looked at him, she felt God speak to her, and she said to the man, "Excuse me, I know you don't know me, but God has said that he has heard your prayer, and you are not to worry, because he is responding to your prayer." He looked at her and burst into tears. As he wiped the tears away, he asked her if she was an angel or a person, and she assured him she was an ordinary woman. Then he told her that that morning he had cried out to God in desperation and asked him to indicate that he had heard by sending an angel to tell him.

There was more. She later walked into the local pub to have some lunch, because that's where she would naturally gravitate to culturally. One of the younger customers knew her. He observed her for a while and then came over, saying, "You're not the person I've known. You have got what I've always wanted. What is it? And how do I obtain it?"

Not knowing quite what to say, she told him he would need to come to Ffald-y-Brenin and talk to us. He had a car, so he drove her back to the center. Because we weren't there, she took him to the chapel. When he entered, the Holy Spirit fell on him, and for several hours nonstop he just cried and cried.

By the time Daphne and I returned, he had gone, but he returned a few days later. He grabbed me by the hand and greeted me. He had rather misunderstood his friend and was convinced I was Father Brendan. (Sometimes people mistake "Ffald-y-Brenin" for "Father Brendan." I usually disabuse them of that notion by introducing my wife to them as "Mother Brendan"!)

Once we had cleared this up, he carried on: "I want to say thanks to you. I just want to say, bless you. I came and spent time in your chapel, and God has come and done something in my life. I just want to say thank you. I'm not the same person; I will never be the same person. Bless you." When God touches people, many of them want to bless others. They've caught the heart of what God is doing here.

A pattern was emerging for us. All we wanted to do was bless. I don't want to judge; I don't want to condemn. I'm not going to approve of sin, but I'm not habitually going to pass judgment on sinners as my first response to them. There will always be times when it is right to share that God has said that sin is sin, but we must declare to sinners that they are known and loved.

Through our blessing of others, we had begun to find that God had a different timetable from ours. As people received blessings, they were often broken and softened and responsive to God. The spirit of conviction then came and revealed directly to their hearts who they were and how they needed God and how they could respond to him. As they began to see how they could be receptors of incredible blessing, of love and mercy, the first thing they wanted to do was change. When they glimpsed something of his presence, it began a process of transformation. Salvation, the initial encounter with God that would lead to the transformation of their lives and the reorientation of their entire thinking and acting, started to spring up at Ffald-y-Brenin.

Alpha courses have become international phenomena. They offer a place for attendees to ask and discuss popular or difficult questions about God over a ten-week period, with one weekend away when the focus turns particularly to the person of the Holy Spirit.

One time a group of students came to us for their Alpha weekend away.

The Alpha group's leaders counted the beds that were available and the students they were bringing and found that they had two too many beds booked! So they decided to bless some friends with a holiday. After some thought, they became convinced that they should invite two particular women—voluble, lifelong atheist friends.

Their atheistic friends suggested they were crazy to invite them to a Christian center but relented when the students promised them they would not have to attend or witness any kind of religious ritual, not even grace at meals.

All went well and boundaries were observed, but at a little after five o'clock on the Saturday, the students doing the Alpha course returned to the center and found the two women waiting for them, seemingly agitated. "Could you please point out the leader?" they asked.

She was located and they continued, "Can you please tell us how we open our hearts to God?"

She expressed surprise given their background, and they countered that they had been wrong.

"How do you know you are wrong?" the leader asked.

They began to explain: "He's here, isn't he? We've just been sitting in his presence all day. We don't know how to respond to it."

The Alpha leader very wisely said, "Go into the chapel. We'll not be anywhere near. Speak to God and ask him to show you how to respond."

So at about half past five they went into the chapel. They were aware of God's presence, but singing and praying were not options that would have sprung to their minds. They had no experience of using the Bible. They just sat there at a bit of a loss.

In the end they just spoke out and said, "We don't know how to respond. We need you to help us. Will you come and help us?" They waited, and the sense of his presence grew. They asked him for more help, and it occurred to one of them to suggest they simply say the name Jesus. All of a sudden they started laughing, because they were overwhelmed with joy. And every time they spoke his name, they were overwhelmed with an incredible joy that just washed over them. They couldn't stand, they were laughing and crying so much. They wanted to burst, they said, with his presence.

At 3:30 in the morning, they lost their voices! This was actually a relief, as people in the rooms around the chapel hadn't been able to sleep because of the noise. The two women thought this kind of experience might happen only in a chapel, so they were unwilling to leave. Instead, they got the cushions off the seating, laid them on the floor and lay there with their hands raised, whispering "Jesus" for the rest of the night. Their lives were transformed, as you can imagine.

One year later, one of the young women returned as the leader of an Alpha group, and the other one was also doing well. Salvation was happening, not just because of verbal persuasion, but because people were encountering God.

He seemed to be delighting in working with what we might call the unlikely ones. One day, a church youth group came to stay. The young people, in their early teens, had always kept their involvement in any church-related activity quiet. They had all agreed to the weekend away if they didn't have to congregate to get on the bus, so they arrived in stages.

On Friday evening the Holy Spirit began to spontaneously fall on them. On Saturday morning they were being baptized in the Spirit one after the other and began to walk in the gifts of the Spirit. The rector's wife, who had organized the weekend, called her husband and said, "I don't care what's in your diary, we need you here. We can't cope with all this. The kids are being filled with the Holy Spirit. We're not doing it; it's just happening." He came, and they worked together to help the children understand what God was showing them.

When the children went to school on Monday they held a lunchtime meeting and created a small committee. The committee was sent on their behalf to the headmaster to ask if it was okay for them to share their faith during breaks and lunch. They also asked if they could start a prayer group, which would pray for all the other children in the school.

The headmaster was astonished. This newfound fervor seemed to come completely out of the blue. They told him, "We've always heard stories about Jesus and most of us have believed stories about Jesus, but we didn't know you could know him personally. He's come to us and we know him and we want all our friends to know him too."

Lest we get too sentimental about this profound story, it's worth noting that these kids didn't become overnight saints. They had an incredible experience of the Holy Spirit, but when they left on Sunday afternoon, a couple of the adults had to stay behind to help mend the beds the kids had wrecked by bouncing on them.

Another time we were approached by an inner-city church, which with some trepidation told us that their young people were wild and a little bizarre. They were not Christians, and they barely spoke to each other or the leaders. One of them was a known drug dealer, another was an addict. When they came for their visit, an adult accompanied each youngster. They arrived in two minibuses after a journey that had been marked by sullen silence.

When they came into the lobby, the youngsters stopped, and one of them turned around and said, "Okay, what's going on here then?"

"What do you mean?" the leaders asked.

"Well, there's something going on here, isn't there?"

They went up and sat down for their meal. Our catering team had been warned that it might be a very tense mealtime, but instead they had a room full of young people laughing and talking to each other nonstop. This was, in hindsight, a sign that God's presence was already changing the situation.

After the meal the leaders told the young people that they wanted to talk to them about who Jesus is. And that was it. They started to fall to the floor, and Jesus began appearing to them in open visions, speaking to them individually. Later they explained what he had said to them, which went something like this:

> I want to talk to you about all the pain in your life. I want to talk to you about everything you're carrying, all the wounds that you've received. I want to tell you that I am here to heal those hurts and take away the pain and set you free so that you can live liberated lives. I have a plan for you, and I want to release it. Now I want you to look at my hands and my feet and my side, and I want you to see my wounds. Well, you didn't deserve the wounds that you have in your heart, and I didn't deserve the wounds that I carried in my body, but I volunteered to have them so that your pain could be dealt with in my pain. I will carry your pain, take it away. If you turn to me, I will heal you and I will forgive you, and I will set you free for life.

And so all of them—not one hesitated—said yes, and then he baptized them all in the Holy Spirit as they lay on the floor. They began to speak in tongues and to worship him and bless him. And then they began to prophesy. It was wonderful. Just wonderful.

We respond to God's activity here by praying:

> Lord, we bless what you do. We love what you do. We bless it, that it can increase, Lord. Keep doing this, Lord. We love what you do. We bless your activity here, Lord. We welcome it even when it appears bizarre. God, we want you to be God, and even if there are some things that make us, a sophisticated people, feel uncomfortable as we think of ourselves, we don't want to limit you, God. You can do whatever you like, even if it offends us. You do what you want to do, God, in the way you want to do it, and we'll bless it.

These wonderful works of the Holy Spirit usually have a foundation that God has chosen to build on. Our foundation had been the simple request that we might be a house of prayer. It was a simple request, but the unfolding of God's response would provide many lessons for us and not a little "wrestling with God."

CHAPTER 3

BECOMING A HOUSE OF PRAYER

The question that had captured my sense of frustration as I reflected on the tension between running a Christian retreat center and wanting to reach the unchurched was "Why am I here?" God gave us an answer as he sent people to us and met with them through prayers of blessing and the sheer wonder of finding themselves in his presence.

As with much of life, however, there is what filmmakers call a backstory. A film will sometimes reference a character's past to make sense of his or her present circumstances. Our backstory both makes sense of what God began to do at Ffald-y-Brenin and releases a sense of wonder at what happened, given our very human meandering toward God's will rather than taking him at his word.

Daphne and I knew we were about to enter a fresh season in our lives in the years before we came to southwest Wales, and as you will read later, we were eventually drawn to Pembrokeshire. Our plans were well in hand when I had an experience that weakened the foundations of my shaky resolve.

About a fortnight before moving here, I had a chance encounter in the street with a Christian leader and minister for whom I have a great deal of respect. We were pleased to see each other, and we exchanged news. He mentioned that he had heard about my new role in Pembrokeshire, and what he said next shook me: "I just want to tell you how sorry I am to hear that. This will be the end of your ministry. It will be the end of anybody ever hearing of you; it will be the end of any influence you might ever have. You've basically walked away from any hope of God ever doing anything with you or through you. I'm very sorry you're going there. I would've thought that you would've been somewhere in the northern Welsh mountains."

Daphne and I had always felt a mission pull to the area he mentioned, so this really disturbed me. For a number of days I just couldn't rest, until in a moment of clarity God moved me on. I reminded myself, "God has said this is where we're to go, so we're going. And if in God's plan that means I'm never useful again, never heard of again, just disappear into nothing, who cares? It is utterly irrelevant. All that matters is whether we're obeying God." This was, if I'm honest, a new place for me to be in: not seeking something for myself, but being abandoned to God's call and his will.

When we arrived at Ffald-y-Brenin, we patiently observed, asked questions, and sought to understand who was visiting the center and why the guests came. It became clear that the reality of center life was a little different from what the trustees perceived it to be.

In those nervous early weeks in a new role, encountering a different version of how things were, latent doubt surfaced. I was asking, "Lord, why are we here?"

And I sensed two responses. I sensed God speaking to me and saying:

> It's because you come here in weakness and cannot minister or move out of your usual experience that I want you here. You have nothing to give, so you have to be abandoned to me. And the fact that your eyes are opened so that you're able to discern what's going on spiritually means that you can see what the evil one is doing and you can deal with it. But you don't know how to, so again, you have no experience with this particular area and you have to come back to me. It's your helplessness that I want.

I was helpless and experiencing a tremendous sense of weakness that I'd never known in my life before. Nevertheless I kept wrestling with God. I cried out and said, "Lord, I have to build a vision here, but I don't know where to start. So, Lord, what is your vision for Ffald-y-Brenin?"

God's response sounded with the clarity of a bell: "Become a house of prayer."

I had no problem with that at all, but my mind soon turned to details. What would Ffald-y-Brenin look like as a house of prayer? What would it mean for Ffald-y-Brenin to become a house of prayer with respect to the locality? We sit on the side of a mountain 600 feet above sea level. We've got another 600 feet going up behind us to the ridge and then a 1,200-foot drop straight to the sea. In front of us we have the valley running below for some miles, rising up on the other side to nearly 1,800 feet. We see sheep everywhere, but very few people. There's no local Christian community that can support such a project.

There is no city or big town locally. Why would this isolated spot be a good place for a house of prayer?

God seems to delight in taking those viewed as weak and vulnerable, such as shepherds and tax collectors, women and children, and showing his strength through them. That God might bless a rural prayer house stretched the imagination but wasn't a total shock. I was more concerned about the realities of a rhythm of prayer and communal life and how that might arise on this remote hillside.

I was no stranger to the idea of 24–7 prayer and harbored a passion and a heart for a place with a rhythm of prayer, where there would be never-ending praise and worship to Jesus, where his presence was manifest, where healing flowed, where teams came in and out, carrying his presence out to the people. I longed for that, but the models I was familiar with didn't seem viable at Ffald-y-Brenin. The 24–7 prayer model of one-hour prayer slots in a dedicated prayer room needs fifty to sixty people to sustain it for a week, let alone months. The Mike Bickle–inspired International House of Prayer model, with its liturgy and worship around the clock, needed that many people a day. Neither seemed an option for us.

Could God do something that was new and rural? Would that rural model spread to urban and city areas? These were the questions that swirled around my mind.

Then people I'd never heard of started calling. They didn't know me by name; they just wanted to speak to whoever was directing the work. "Have you ever thought of turning Ffald-y-Brenin into a house of prayer?" they asked.

We didn't actually feel that God was calling us away from being a retreat center. We just knew that being a house of prayer should be part of the character of the center. I listened patiently to several insistent callers and their offers of help, but I was hearing the same message each time: set a room aside, obtain a collection of flags for every nation, and have boards or holders for briefing notes. In one case a person said he could supply the prayer room in a box for £360 (over $550)! I had no problem with the method, and assured the callers that I was praying that God would bless and prosper their prayer rooms, but I wasn't actually looking for their help; nor did I want to adopt their methods. Furnishing a room physically was not what God was calling Ffald-y-Brenin to do.

So we persisted in prayer and before long God began to unfold his wisdom: "Roy, if Ffald-y-Brenin is going to become a house of prayer, first of all you must become a house of prayer yourself."

That challenged me. I had long been full of zeal to bring people to the Lord and to help restore broken relationships between people and God. My prayer life, however, was urgent and hurried. I would be on my way to a meeting or an appointment, praying passionately that the power of God would anoint my words and give me wisdom and insight. But that was it. Being more reflective or spending time simply being available to hear from God did occur to me, but I was always too busy to implement my well-meaning plans.

Not long after this, during our morning worship in chapel, the psalm of the day was Psalm 42, and verse 4 came alive to me:

These things I remember
as I pour out my soul:
how I used to go with the multitude,
leading the procession to the house of God,
with shouts of joy and thanksgiving
among the festive throng.

I found myself thinking back to the late seventies and early eighties, when it seemed as though the Holy Spirit was being poured out like a torrent and many were being converted. I remembered an evening in Birmingham Central Hall, led by Trevor Dearing, where God touched many powerfully during the meeting. In the end the caretakers came on the stage and stopped the meeting and said, "I'm sorry, but you're already an hour and a half past your finishing time, and we just have to clean the hall because we have people coming in tomorrow."

Hundreds and hundreds of people streamed out of the meeting and down Corporation Street toward the bus or train station. Many of them were carrying crutches over their shoulders—the crutches they'd walked in on. Others were carrying or pushing folded-up wheelchairs that they'd been brought in on. Hundreds of people in the city-center streets spontaneously burst into hymns and songs of praise.

As the memories cascaded through my waking dream, I found myself saying, "Oh Lord God, how I miss you. How I miss you moving like that." To my amazement I heard God reply:

Oh Roy, how I miss the relationship we had then.
How I remember those days when you would stop,

and you would worship me, and you would sing to
me and honor me, all those years ago. How I miss
you, Roy. How I wish that we had that back again.
How I miss that openness to me that you had.

It took my breath away. I was so stirred up I had to act. I invited
a couple of people who were working with us to come and join
Daphne and me in our kitchen. I asked them to be witnesses of my
confession to God and my resolve from that day on. I told them that
even after thirty years of ministry I did not know how to pray.

One of them started to laugh at me and scoff, and I said, "Please
don't do that. This is me from the heart. This is the real me." Then I
knelt on the floor in front of them, and I prayed aloud so they could
witness what I was saying: "Lord God, I want to say to you that the
truth is I do not know how to pray. If I knew how to pray, life would
be so different. But the truth is, I don't."

Now all I actually expected to happen, and all I wanted, was to
ensure that I'd put a marker down again. I'd raised the stones of an
altar, a memorial, and there were witnesses, human witnesses, who
would always remind me of what I had done.

What actually happened was that the Lord spoke to me very
clearly: "Roy, I've been waiting for years for you to say that. May I
begin to teach you now? I want you to walk across the land, I want
you to go into the buildings and I want you to pray through all the
buildings, and this is how I want you to pray...." And he gave me
specific instructions on how and what to pray. It was biblical in content, but it wasn't a style of praying I'd ever adopted or experienced,
so I shared it with Daphne and the other two, and we went over to

the main center. It was a lovely sunny day and all the guests were out for the afternoon. We went through the whole building, room by room, and they joined me in praying in the way that God had instructed me.

He had said three things. First of all, to pray the name of Jesus into the fabric of every room and into the air, the atmosphere of the room, but call on the blood of Jesus, and press the blood of Jesus into everything in the room. This meant the ceiling, the floor, the walls, the doors, the windows, and the furniture. So we had to get a stepladder so we could reach the ceilings and lay hands on them and figuratively press the blood of Jesus into them.

We then walked the land, all thirty acres, and said, "We call on the blood of Jesus and the name of Jesus. We glorify and lift up and exalt the name of Jesus, and we press the blood of Jesus into the land, so it covers every curse, every sin, every other form of bloodshed that has happened here in the past. Every wounding, we cover it with the blood of Jesus and we press the blood of Jesus into the land."

The third thing he said was that we were to pray that things would be straightened in the buildings. Well, we didn't have a clue what that meant. And one of the physical aspects of the buildings here is that it's very difficult to find a straight line, or a straight wall, where walls meet floors. They're not straight. There are no square windows. But there was something spiritual going on here and we needed to do this, whether we fully understood it or not. So that's how we prayed, and it released tremendous blessing.

It was easy to do in most of the rooms, but in several areas it was very difficult to break through into ease of prayer and worship. There was strong resistance and we needed to call on the name and the blood of Jesus and dispel any stubborn resistance. And we had to stay a while and pray more, so that those rooms were clean of whatever seemed to be contaminating them spiritually.

We had just finished the last room when the first car appeared at the head of the drive with returning guests. We quickly moved out of the way and later that night went to bed content that we'd done what God had told us to do.

Early the next morning there was a frantic hammering on our front door, and we emerged to find the guests—who had come as individuals and not as a group—up and talking. I thought maybe the fire alarm had gone off, but it turned out that there was a different kind of fire at work.

During the night, Jesus had appeared in dreams to each of them and spoken amazing words individually to them, into their lives and their situations, and for each of them this had brought amazing healing. In many cases his words had touched concerns that nobody else knew about, in their childhood, very early on in their lives. There was wonderful healing and a new freedom for them all.

Now they wanted an explanation, and our pithy response to these thirty overwhelmed guests was "God is blessing you. Let's just give him thanks, and let's ask him to keep blessing you."

That wasn't all. In the following weeks a torrent of water began flowing out of springs above us that had been dry for many years. It was their dryness that had given rise to the name of the area here: Sychbant, which means "dry streambed." The millstream that had been fed by the springs had dried up and was no more. But now there was a torrent of water.

In the local paper the inexplicable rise of the water table in the Preselis, the name for the local district, was headline news. The National Park Authority needed to liaise with the Environment Agency on this new development. There was an issue to do with surface water on the deforested hill above us, so they asked if they could hold the meeting at Ffald-y-Brenin and invited me to sit in. I felt this was God neatly showing us what was being restored as a result of our prayers.

God was slowly increasing the pace by asking us to do things that took us outside our comfort zone and our natural way of thinking. One way he did this was to provoke me to raise up prayer for Pembrokeshire. This was a challenge, because we'd only been here a short time. We really didn't know many people at all, and we hadn't known anybody when we first arrived. We hardly knew where to start. It also felt a little odd that as newcomers we were trying to stir up countywide prayer. But God seemed to be very clear and very insistent, so we mentioned it to a few people, and very soon other people contacted us, wanting to be part of this new network of prayer.

We invited people to commit one hour a week for fifty-two weeks. During that hour they would spend their time simply praying to God and asking him to come and bless Pembrokeshire. The first hours to be taken were those between two o'clock and seven o'clock in the morning. Not by younger people but by older people, who reasoned that they were often awake during the night anyway and prayer might be a productive use of that time.

After a time of planning, we launched and prayed for twelve months, with an average of ten hours' prayer per weekday being taken up by our band of praying people. Many were not used to praying for an hour, so we created a simple menu of prayer.

We suggested that people pray what the ancients called a prayer of examen, but we simply called it "the starter": "Lord, I'm in Pembrokeshire. Before I can ask your blessings, I need to be sure that I'm clean and that I'm walking in your blessing." We encouraged people to confess anything that needed to be confessed so that they would be ready and able to receive the blessings that God wanted to give them.

Then there was "the main course," which was praying for Pembrokeshire. There was an array of suggestions within that, covering political, social, and spiritual issues. We had prayer suggestions for neighborhoods and neighbors. It was also important to pray for churches, fellowships, and leaders in their area.

And then there was "dessert," which involved praying for the nation. This covered the national assembly and justice, economic, and employment issues.

"Coffee" was blessing the person you were about to hand the watch on to. You called that person, blessed them, and then passed the watch to them (unless it was three o'clock in the morning and the person who was going to pray had a spouse who would be fast asleep!).

Many of the people had never prayed like this before and found this depth of prayer new and refreshing. But it was also wonderful for Pembrokeshire, as many churches found their liberal ministers suddenly leaving and being replaced with really good, sound, spiritually alive people with hearts to work with others.

We felt strongly that the mandate to do this was for fifty-two weeks only, so as the final weeks arrived, we invited people up to the center and told them the project was going to end. Although some were secretly relieved that their 4:00 a.m. praying schedule was over, some were adamant that they were going to carry on. We didn't want to stand in their way, but we made it clear we wouldn't coordinate it anymore. As the conversation unfolded, some talked about their friends outside Pembrokeshire who wanted to do a similar thing. I felt prompted to share about the commitment Daphne and I had made to pray for Wales every day and ask if anyone would like to join us.

Now we had thirty-two people who wanted to ask God to bless Wales every day. They wanted some more prayer starters, so I agreed to see what could be done. As I spent time with God, I was moved to write down what has become known as the Caleb Prayer:

> O High King of heaven,
> Have mercy on our land.
> Revive your church;
> Send the Holy Spirit
> For the sake of the children.
> May your kingdom come to our nation.
> In Jesus' mighty name. Amen.

You could simply pray it through in fifteen seconds, or you could find yourself caught by a particular word, phrase, or sentence and spend longer praying about what God was saying through that word or line.

Our initial thirty-two grew within two months to five hundred. People we didn't know were calling or emailing and asking for copies of the prayer. One minister asked for fifty copies. A month later he wrote again and asked if he could have another fifty. I called him and asked how many people he had in his congregation. He told me twelve, so I said, "Well, if you don't mind me asking, why do you want a hundred copies?" His answer was poignant: "God has spoken to me, gripped me. I'm moving around the churches and chapels, calling people to make this commitment, and when they do, I'm giving them a copy of the prayer." Soon there were over a thousand copies in circulation, and we gave up trying to record who had taken up the Caleb Prayer commitment.

A little while later we had a call out of the blue from a local radio station. They wanted to interview me about what God was doing at Ffald-y-Brenin. Toward the end of the interview the reporter asked if they could record the Caleb Prayer in English and in Welsh, so I prayed in English, Daphne in Welsh. Then the interviewer asked whether we would mind if they broadcast it across the county twice a day for a week!

We began to hear more stories about the impact of the prayer. One man went door to door in his area, asking people, "Are you concerned for your children and for their future? Are you concerned about young people in the area and their rowdiness and their lack of direction? Would you like quiet and calm to come to these streets so that this might be a place where children have a future and young people have a hope?" Many nonchurchgoers responded and began to discover a connection with God as they prayed each day.

Not long after this a national prayer meeting was called on the Royal Welsh Showground. The day was structured around the Caleb

Prayer, with each session taking a clause or sentence as the starting point for prayer.

We then became aware that people were prayer walking around their towns, using the prayer as the framework for calling God's blessing on their local communities. We just listened and marveled, but there was more to come. We started getting copies of the prayer written in other languages coming to us from people in other nations who were using it. We began to get calls from people who had only just discovered where the prayer came from but had already sent it out around the world. "What will the copyright fee be?" was their worried question. We would laugh and reassure them that there was no fee and that we were happy the prayer was being used around the world.

In the meantime, in desperation, Daphne and I were crying out to God, saying, "When is Ffald-y-Brenin going to be a house of prayer? What will it look like as a house of prayer? Why is nothing happening?"

At this point we had stirred thousands of people regarding prayer, but we hadn't connected this to the idea that the center was to be a house of prayer. Then one morning there was an email newsletter from America in my inbox. I read through it and was struck by an article about an initiative that was taking place in Namibia. It grabbed my attention because one or two things reported in the article sounded rather like the situation we faced in Wales. Both nations seemed to be like a wilderness spiritually.

I wasn't sure where Namibia was, and I certainly didn't know anything about it, so I got hold of the Patrick Johnstone book on praying for the world, *Operation World*, and looked it up. I noticed many similarities between the two nations.

I emailed the sender of the newsletter in the States and said that I felt God speaking to me about the Namibian situation and asked if he had any sort of contact he could email me. I had a reply within five minutes with some information.

I emailed the contact, explaining how I'd been stirred up about the revival heritage of our nations and the current spiritual need. I shared about how God had been using the Caleb Prayer and said that if it would be useful to them they should feel free to use it, and I hoped I hadn't offended them by this unsolicited email.

As I wrote, I felt so aware of God's heartbeat in it, but it was to be three weeks before I heard back. By that point I had begun to wonder if maybe I had gotten my guidance completely wrong. This is what I read when the response came:

> I need to tell you what's happening here. You don't know who I am, but I'm the national coordinator of a new movement for reconciliation in Namibia. I've been set aside to move the Namibian church to unite together in a day of reconciliation, of open repentance for our divisions, for the poor witness that we have been and the things that we've said to each other.
>
> It's a day when we're going to humble ourselves nationally before the nation, and ask God to bless us. Three weeks ago we had a council meeting, and for the first time in a generation, all the leaders of the churches and streams in the nation came together. We prayed and sought God together. In the last

session, we were astonished when a Pentecostal leader stood up and said: "This is God's message: I'm going to send you a prayer from outside of Africa, so that none of you can claim to own it, and you're going to pray it and I'm going to respond to it."

Their sessions together came to a close and nobody had a clue what this prophecy referred to. My friend went on holiday with his family and during that time sought to understand from God what "a prayer from outside of Africa" meant. On his return he opened his emails and there was my rather tentative suggestion.

I was invited to attend the resulting Day of Repentance and Reconciliation, but I couldn't get a flight. There was, however, international press coverage of the day of prayer and how the churches had repented before the nation, humbled themselves, and prayed something called the Caleb Prayer together.

However, I still wasn't joining the dots with respect to the house of prayer promise for Ffald-y-Brenin and remained desperate for answers. As I searched the Scriptures, I found myself immersed in Isaiah 56 for a while, a chapter with many key insights about what being a house of prayer might mean:

This is what the LORD says:

"Maintain justice
    and do what is right,
for my salvation is close at hand

and my righteousness will soon be revealed.
Blessed is the man who does this,
    the man who holds it fast,
who keeps the Sabbath without desecrating it,
    and keeps his hand from doing any evil."

Let no foreigner who has bound himself to the LORD
say,
    "The LORD will surely exclude me from his people."
And let not any eunuch complain,
    "I am only a dry tree."

For this is what the LORD says:

"To the eunuchs who keep my Sabbaths,
    who choose what pleases me
    and hold fast to my covenant—
to them I will give within my temple and its walls
    a memorial and a name
    better than sons and daughters;
I will give them an everlasting name
    that will not be cut off.
And foreigners who bind themselves to the LORD
    to serve him,
to love the name of the LORD,
    and to worship him,
all who keep the Sabbath without desecrating it
    and who hold fast to my covenant—

these I will bring to my holy mountain
and give them joy in my house of prayer.
Their burnt offerings and sacrifices
will be accepted on my altar;
for my house will be called
a house of prayer for all nations."

Those who are divided, those who have no future, those who have no status, those who have no children, no name, or are simply not from the family of Israel, come together in the house of prayer and find joy.

As we grasped this, the events of the previous weeks and months began to have implications for the house of prayer vision. We had a rhythm of prayer that we had established in Ffald-y-Brenin, and growing numbers of people were coming to pray. We had helped establish a year of prayer for our locality and had seen thousands of people in different nations and language groups, on different continents, stirred up in prayer movements using the Caleb Prayer resource. Vision and practical aids were going around the world from this tiny, insignificant, remote, and obscure place on a Welsh hillside.

God was showing us what it meant for us to be a house of prayer. Testimonies of life were coming out of the lips of people who had come here. They were finding healing and restoration and direction. They were finding Jesus. They were being filled with the Holy Spirit. They were full of joy.

God impressed on us that the center needed to be a place of reconciliation for those caught up in conflict. It also needed to welcome those who had run out of hope. It had to be a place where those who were long in the tooth in their Christian walk, dried up and exhausted, could come and find rest and restoration.

We started crying out to God that he would bring those people. As usual the answers were not long in coming. Then we asked about the nations. We sensed God saying, "What do you want me to do?" We asked him to bring the nations to us.

Sometime later we checked our visitors' book for the previous six months and realized that we had had visitors staying here from eighteen different nations. Some of their stories were astonishing and some of their insights were to help us move on to the next stage of what God had in store for us.

At about eleven o'clock one night I heard a knock on our door, and there stood two white-faced, absolutely exhausted people. I had been expecting two guests much earlier in the day and was half-expecting them not to come.

Tall, fiftysomething, and looking as if they needed sleep, they readily assented when I suggested I take them straight to their room. As we walked, I asked them where they had come from. They had come from Jerusalem that day—they had thought the journey from Heathrow would be quicker! They then asked for supper, despite being self-catering guests (they had misunderstood the term *self-catering*). I found them food by raiding our larder and then said good night to them.

It had not been the most promising encounter, but when they had stood at the door, I had sensed a stirring from the Holy Spirit. Halfway through the following morning they were back at our door, bright eyed and bushy tailed but seemingly about to leave. They just wanted to say hello. I invited them in for a coffee but very quickly began to feel overcome by the Spirit, which rather militated against my coffee-making efforts.

During the flow of the conversation one of the guests stopped and said, "Do you know why we're here?" I said that I didn't and carried on pouring the coffee, then sat down. Later, he stopped again and said, "Do you know why we're here?" Again I answered, "No." And then he just picked up his conversation. The third time he said, "Do you know why we're here?" I replied, "No. Do you?" He said he did.

I was finding myself in a situation where my instinct was to become defensive. I was rather scared by the unknown aspects of the situation. I didn't know these people, didn't know what "spirit" they were moving in, didn't know anything, really, except their names. I was open but wary.

He continued, "We run a 24–7 prayer house in Israel. We heard about you through somebody from Israel who visited you. Two weeks ago God spoke to us, and he said we were to get on a plane, come here, ask for you, and speak some words to you."

My mental defenses moved to level 2 alert. Why would God send someone from Jerusalem to southwest Wales to speak to me? This person didn't sound very sane to me. However, I encouraged him to continue, and he indicated that he wanted to share a scripture. I began to relax, but I was still having a side conversation with God in my head: *Lord Jesus, I call on you to protect me, your angels to surround me. Holy Spirit, cover me; the blood of Jesus cover every part of me. But I want to hear anything you have to say.*

Then the man said, "Actually, I want to sing the words. Is that okay?" (Level 3 alarms go off internally.) I managed a smile and said yes.

He began to sing the Aaronic Blessing from Numbers: "The LORD bless you and keep you; the LORD make his face to shine upon you and be gracious to you; the LORD lift up his countenance upon you and give you peace" (6:24–26 ESV).

I didn't know anything about this man. I didn't know if he was a musician by background, and he sang so quietly, but his voice reverberated through the whole house as he declared, "The Lord bless you." Then he looked at me and said, "That was just to prepare you for what God wants to say to you. We've come from Jerusalem to tell you that the Lord blesses you from out of Zion." The couple lived on Mount Zion.

It took my breath away. It seemed wonderful to me that God would send someone all the way from Jerusalem to speak such poignant words of blessing. It was as though God were saying to me, "You see, I do know you, watch over you, and care for you and about you." I had not realized how much I needed that sense of affirmation, and it increased my sense of being placed for a purpose. It was as though grace were being poured out when I thought I had already received as much grace as I could handle. Psalm 20:2 reads, "May he send you help from the sanctuary and give you support from Zion!" (ESV).

There was more, however. They produced a map and asked how to pronounce the name of a little town in Mid-Wales. God had told them to go there, but they didn't know who they were supposed to meet. I did, however! A prayer room had recently been started up at the back of a Christian bookshop. Daphne and I had just been to see the people involved and to bless what they were doing. So the couple went up there, met them, and blessed their new venture.

Daphne was away, and I think maybe that was in God's timing, because that night I shook so much under the power of God that I nearly fell out of the bed. God breathed something into me that night. He was calling his people back to prayer. They needed to reconnect with him before they went out to harvest. He was looking for simplicity and purity—not in a legalistic sense, but in a rekindling of relationship. Our lives had become full of meetings, many of which were good and helpful but lacking in real connection with the Father. I sensed him saying:

> I want to look them in the eye and I want them
> to look me in the eye and I want us to have love
> meetings and joy meetings and acceptance meet-
> ings. I want my people to be people who come
> for hugs, and I want them to call me Father from
> their heart. I want to be able to speak to them
> by name and tell them how much I love them,
> how much I delight in them. I want to grow that
> relationship.

I received an open vision that showed a great release of home-based experience of the work of the Holy Spirit. There was a transformation happening for people. A healing of acceptance and recognition for those who didn't think they would ever be recognized. Fire and passion characterized people's lives.

Instead of there being simply hundreds and hundreds of churches ablaze for the Lord across the land, there were also thousands upon thousands of homes that were ablaze for the Lord.

Communities were affected. The nation was ablaze with the fire of the Holy Spirit poured out through homes and churches.

I found myself pleading with God: "Lord, teach me more about how to pray in the way you want me to pray. I've been a Christian for decades, Lord, but I'm still at the first steps of learning about prayer. I want to relinquish the models of prayer that I've been taught either by reading about them or by observing them in the lives of other people. Lord, what does it mean for me to be a praying person?"

The Bible calls us to pray but rarely suggests the methods. How could we discover patterns of prayer that reflected the heart of God rather than the methods of man? God had more for us as we continued on this voyage of discovery.

Sometimes guests can be with us for a week and we hardly see them. One guest came to her first chapel service on her final morning. She asked to see us afterward, and we retired to our kitchen to talk. She was Australian and had Welsh family roots. Her grandfather had been a miner and a drunkard and had abused his wife. There was never enough money to pay for food, and life was desperate for the family. So his wife did an almost unheard-of thing in the society of that time: she ran away with her daughter to Australia. The bitterness about Wales was passed on to her daughter and to the child she had when she got married.

That child now sat in our kitchen. Pat had become a Christian and eventually became a worker with Youth With A Mission (YWAM). She soon discovered 24–7 prayer and spent time at the International House of Prayer (IHOP) in Kansas. God began to speak to her, prompting her to visit the land of her fathers. She didn't want to go, but God was insistent. He supplied the money in response to her prayers, and she arrived for a cold, wet week in Wales. Her hatred for Wales was not diminishing.

On her last full day she discovered that the pit where her grandfather had worked was now an open museum, so she decided to take a tour and found herself in the depths of the pit. The tour guide demonstrated what it had been like for the men who worked there by switching off the lights. The visitors were plunged into a blackness relieved only by an occasional candle.

Two things happened simultaneously. She became aware of the enormity and blackness of sin in a way she'd never experienced before, and she was also suddenly aware of the environment in which her grandfather had worked every day of his working life to support his family. He set out to walk to work in the dark, he worked in darkness, and he walked home in the darkness. He rarely saw light. "If I worked and lived like this I would probably turn to drink as well," she reasoned as the tears began to flow. She wept and repented of all the judgment she'd carried in her heart over her grandfather.

As she was about to leave, the tears still flowing down her face, she was approached by a man called Roland, who asked, "Excuse me, but are you a Christian?" He gave her a plastic bag with coal in it, which she accepted a little warily. He continued, "This is Welsh coal that was in the land during the years of revival in this nation, and I want to give it to you." She accepted his gift, even as she continued to weep.

Pat returned to Australia and was busy with a prayer room project over the next three weeks. Back at her home church for the first time she asked if she could give her testimony. She shared the story of her repentance toward Wales and toward her grandfather and her roots. And then she explained about the coal. She opened the bag and poured out the pieces of coal, and as she did, the Holy Spirit fell on the congregation.

For three months it was like everything you read of the 1904–1905 revival in Wales. Nonchurchgoing people were pouring into the church, crying out in repentance. Others were falling down in their workplaces under conviction. Prayer meetings and worship were lasting all night, and many, many people were coming to the Lord.

A year later, God spoke to Pat in an unexpected way and said, "You are to go back to Wales and you will experience joy there. You are to take the coal back with you to Wales because it was only on loan."

But she wasn't clear what she was to do with it. Was she to take it to a pit and return it to the ground? She had heard of Ffald-y-Brenin, so she came here to pray and seek the Lord. While she was here, God said to her, "This is where you are to leave the coal. Tell the story and give them the coal."

In the months that followed, I shared her story wherever I went and then opened the bag of coal. This symbolic action was often followed by evidence of grace and blessing as the Holy Spirit began touching those present. Our sense of what it meant to be a house of prayer was growing as these signs from the Father accumulated.

We felt prompted to bring the local community, the eighty or so people from the valley and local hillsides, together for a meal. As we puzzled and prayed as to what might encourage them to come, we became aware that a bishop in north Wales had been born in our valley, so Daphne called him with a date several months away in mind. His response was swift: "This is God at work. I'm coming in three weeks' time." He then told us where we would meet and what would happen. We were a bit nonplussed at this turn of events, but we started the word-of-mouth process and sixty-eight people arrived and were fed. We still felt a little insecure. The whole evening was in Welsh apart from the interview with me. We didn't know enough about the bishop to know where he stood spiritually. Was everything going to be okay?

It came to his turn to speak and he turned to the people and said:

> This is what I want to talk to you about. I want to talk to you about the Trinity. There is a little Anglican church in the valley, and that speaks of generations, of history, of lasting, of establishment. All of these things speak to us of the Father.
>
> There's a Baptist chapel here as well, with a baptistery, and this speaks to us of the Son, who has come and called us to repentance, and our need to be baptized internally and externally.
>
> Ffald-y-Brenin has been placed in our midst as a sign of the Holy Spirit. The breath of God is moving at Ffald-y-Brenin, and I want to say to you openly that the winter has passed for southwest Wales. The spring has started.

We were utterly astonished at what he said. A local Welsh language secular newspaper told its readers: "Well-known bishop says the winter of the church in southwest Wales is over, springtime has come, bulbs are appearing in the land."

We had so nearly not come to this hillside of blessing, resisting God and his prompting. But God had other ideas about our destiny.

CHAPTER 4

TALES OF A RELUCTANT CENTER DIRECTOR

The seeds of the events you have been reading about so far were planted in the difficult years before we arrived, somewhat reluctantly, at Ffald-y-Brenin. I had been broken by the collapse of a business project involving betrayal by a business partner and poor choices. My personal integrity had been called into account and found wanting. Shame sat on my shoulders and claimed me for its own. It was clear to me that I had no future in God's purposes as far as ministry was concerned. There seemed to be no way forward for my life.

One day I was chatting with Peter Middlemiss, who was the director of a retreat center in Evesham, Worcestershire. He told me that God's plan for my future might involve working with a retreat center. I tried not to laugh in front of him and later reflected with Daphne that perhaps Peter didn't know me very well, despite our well-established friendship. I was in no frame of mind to think about such a job, and I had had no experience of the spiritual traditions that tended to value retreat and contemplation.

Peter had suggested that we check the job ads in the *Church of England Newspaper* (CEN), but for several months I ignored his wise advice. Finally, as desperation began to appear on my personal horizon, I started to check the paper, only to cancel our order later, as there didn't appear to be anything suitable after some weeks of diligent scanning. When the last issue arrived, I saw a job vacancy ad for a couple in a retreat center in Wales. We were curious, but our "no retreat centers" stance remained firmly in place.

I wanted to know more about what God was doing in Wales, a place we both loved, so I suggested to Daphne that we get the information on that basis. In due course a package came and I encountered God in our kitchen as I stood transfixed, reading the brochure and related material. We had just returned from a walk in the hills with our daughter, and warm cups of tea and soft chairs were the order of the day for everyone else. But I remained in the kitchen, muddy boots still on my feet, and as I read of the roots of Ffald-y-Brenin, I was aware of the Holy Spirit's presence in a way I hadn't felt for a long time. God was at work in the Welsh hills, and it stirred my spirit.

However, the job ad hadn't really told the story of what they needed. It was clear that the first stage of the vision for the center was in place. Following the death of Peter Mould, who had established and managed the trust, a new couple were being sought to bring vision, direction, and structure for the future, but no salary was available. They had no money; nor did we. The stirring provoked by the first few pages was being dampened.

There were other negatives too. It was in Pembrokeshire, but our heart had always been for the Welsh mountains, where we had spent a great deal of our leisure time. We saw Pembrokeshire as an English-speaking area, but we wanted to live in a Welsh-speaking area. (We later discovered that Ffald-y-Brenin is in north Pembrokeshire, which is Welsh speaking.)

Nevertheless I was so stirred in my spirit that I actually called up straight away and said that I just wanted to say thank you, to acknowledge that we had received the information, and to tell them how encouraged I was and how clear it was that God was at work with them, but at the moment that was as far as I wanted to go.

Several weeks later it occurred to me that we had left a loose end, and after confirming with Daphne that she didn't want to pursue the vacancy, I wrote to the center to say that this was not something that we could connect with but we wished them well. Neither of us was qualified in any way to lead a retreat center. At an obvious common-sense level Daphne and I were not the people they were looking for.

Shortly afterward, rather to my surprise, I was offered a lucrative commercial job. It involved going to London for an initial week's training. It was a consultancy position, which was the kind of work I had always really enjoyed, and there was a small but very welcome golden hello, as well as substantial rewards in due course if all went well.

Daphne hates me going to London because she knows how much I love it. Invariably when I go there and stay, I give her a call and say that we've just got to move there. Daphne is a thoroughly country girl and could not contemplate coping with that. She was happy I was going to be there for only a week.

I was encouraged by the thought of personal progress and financial security, and turned up at the office block near Heathrow airport for initial training, feeling a degree of optimism. We started at 10:30 and took a coffee break at 11:15. But by then I was feeling very uncomfortable with myself, despite my earlier positive frame of mind, and couldn't pinpoint why. As the day progressed, I grew more disturbed and realized that what I was experiencing was an incredible lack of God's presence. This wasn't a mild stirring or a faint unease. It felt as though an abyss had opened up and I was about to fall into it: it was hellish. The lunch hour felt like a fortnight. After a bar snack in a local pub, I wandered the streets trying to work out what to do. The afternoon was even worse.

Sometimes we talk about being in the wrong paragraph on the page, and occasionally we talk about being in the wrong chapter, but I felt as though I was in the wrong book. At the end of the day I sat in the car for ninety minutes as my mind churned over, and I tried to think of a way out of the trap I found myself in. I knew I was in the wrong place, but I had already spent some of the money from the golden hello on ordinary bills and the expenses of my trip. I couldn't repay the money I'd already received, and the prospect of a big income kept surfacing in my mind. Our daughter was getting married in several weeks, and we needed the money that I was about to earn. I didn't feel that I could leave, but staying meant an absence of God. My head was going round and round like the cars on the busy London roundabout that lay beyond the car park.

Eventually I found a phone box and called Daphne, who was just getting ready to go out. I blurted out my despairing conclusions and said that I was coming home, because I was in the wrong place. It was not easy to tell her. This job had seemed like a remarkable supply of income and security for us as a couple. We were going to have a better lifestyle than we had ever known.

We talked some more, and then Daphne said to me, "You must decide what you think is right and do whatever you think is right in God and I'll support you." This wasn't exactly what I wanted to hear, because I wanted someone else to make the decision for me.

After an hour of aimless driving, I made a decision. I'd rather have God than money. I know now that God put me into that position to force me to make a choice that went to the heart of who I really was, what I was like, and whether I was willing to trust God. He was preparing me by helping me shed the conventional wisdom that had prompted me to put money before ministry in the past. But I had reached the point where I was willing to walk away and choose nothing as long as I had God, so I drove the two hundred miles home.

I was really concerned about the fact that I couldn't repay all the money I'd already been given. The next morning at 9:00 I called the managing director. He remembered me and knew that I had been there the previous day. I told him I was now at home, and he asked what had happened. I wasn't sure he would understand my dealings with God, so I carefully explained: "I discovered very quickly for me that I was the wrong person in the wrong place at the wrong time, and I decided I needed to leave." Somewhat unexpectedly he complimented me on my maturity and good faith and said that the whole experience would help give me clarity for the future. He had to rush to a meeting, but his final words were "I want you to know that we will always speak very well of you, and I hope you will always speak very well of us. By the way, I hope you enjoy the money. Good-bye."

I sat there stunned. A prayer walk seemed to be a good idea, so I set off around the local lanes on a three-mile route, where I rarely saw a vehicle. If I'm honest, these walks had seemed to be marked by the absence of God rather than his presence, but that morning as I set out, I said aloud, "Oh Lord," and instantly I felt as though he were walking at my right hand, and I was aware of him just saying, "Yes?"

I stopped for a moment. What I wanted to do, and what I would do if it were now, because I would be bolder as I think I know him better, was to say, "Where have you been for the last couple of years?" It was not prayer as normal for me that day. I told God the following:

> Lord, I have sought your purpose for my life. I've messed up my life, and I accept responsibility for that, but I've looked at the future and I've seized responsibility for my future and I've done all the responsible things. I've found a door and I've walked through the door, and there was much reward but it wasn't what you wanted for me. So having spent years telling other people that they must take responsibility for their lives, I'm now saying to you that I abrogate my responsibility. I refuse to accept responsibility for my future now. I'm giving it all to you.
>
> I'm not going to do anything except wait for you. I might lose everything, but I'm going to wait for you. I might starve, but I'm going to wait for you. It may take several years, but I'm going to wait for you. I might sink into depression, but I'm going

to wait for you. I'm going to trust you. What I want
you to do, Lord, is be the one who opens the door.
Will you open the door?

The moment I said "Will you open the door?" it was as though
a gale of the Holy Spirit blew in. For the next two and a half miles I
said with every step, "Lord, open the door." It was a simple heartfelt
prayer.

When I arrived back at the door of our house, I could hear the
phone ringing. It was one of the trustees from Ffald-y-Brenin. I was
surprised to hear from them and a little annoyed at having my time
with God interrupted. She inquired how I was and offered me an
update on the recruitment process. I didn't really want to know, but
politeness prevailed.

The trust had advertised and shortlisted a number of people.
Then they had invited them to come together for a long weekend
with the trustees so that their gifts could be assessed and they could
observe the realities of the center.

The trustees met together on the Friday evening to pray. As they
prayed, God gave them a message for me. As she told me this, I was
thinking, *More Christians with funny messages. I wish you'd go away so
I can just have a good time with God.*

She was trying to find the right words to help her recount the
rest of the story. She went on to tell me that God had told them to
send all the candidates home, not to recruit anybody else or look for
anybody else. God further instructed them to call me on a specific
date at 11:00 a.m. with the message "God says this is the place where
he has opened the door."

I didn't want to believe this was happening, and my inner rationalist was working overtime to try to explain this clear guidance. The husband part of my brain was wondering how on earth I was going to tell Daphne. I quietly reassured the woman on the phone that I would talk to Daphne and call back.

When Daphne came home, I prepared the way with a cup of tea before recounting the events of the day. She was a little agitated. In fact, I'm sure they heard her several miles away yelling out, "No, I'm not going. This is not for us."

Daphne and I eventually talked about it some more, and actually the situation was still the same: we didn't have any money, Ffald-y-Brenin didn't have any money, and we had no experience or understanding of retreat centers that would enable us to work with Ffald-y-Brenin.

But we were persuaded to at least visit, and during that visit I was discerning things that were going on in and around Ffald-y-Brenin at both a social level and a spiritual level that were not good. It only reinforced my resistance to the idea of going there. We were invited to visit again and meet with the chair of trustees while we were there, so some weeks later we paid a second visit, and we enjoyed it even less than the first. We were, however, making a good impression and were asked to formally apply. We declined to do so, but we stayed in touch with those we had met. As we continued praying, to my real surprise God spoke to me, saying, "I am calling you to Ffald-y-Brenin, but I'm calling you to more than Ffald-y-Brenin. I'm going to place you, and I'm going to do something in Ffald-y-Brenin that is much more than a retreat center. And I'm placing you there to release it."

Humanly speaking this seemed impossible. But I do know God's voice, so I was prepared to consider the idea. What I struggled to cope with was his mercy in saying to me that he would place me somewhere, because I don't really think I was placing priority in God's purposes. It was utterly undeserved, utterly unexpected, and out of the blue. It just pulled me closer into God's heart. I wanted to know so much more of this God who would have such mercy on me.

A new resolve had entered my life. Instead of talking about him and preaching about him and evangelizing about him and being a pastor for him, I wanted to know God. And now that's my heart: to know him and to know him more. Not to know more about him, but to know him more. Everything else follows as an overflow of that relationship. When the major passion of my heart changed from mission to simply knowing him, the mission activity then began to flow out of the knowing.

With this in mind, I'm fascinated by Jesus' summary of the Law in Matthew 22:37–40: "'Love the Lord your God with all your heart and with all your soul and with all your mind.' This is the first and greatest commandment. And the second is like it: 'Love your neighbor as yourself.' All the Law and the Prophets hang on these two commandments."

Mark made it clear in his gospel that when Jesus called the disciples, it was (a) to be with him and (b) to go (Mark 3:14). This is fleshing out Jesus' summary of the Law and it's to do with the heart, not with obedience to a set of rules. It's a new heart and a new way of relating to God; a new way of seeing the world and creation and all that is in it and God's heart toward his creation.

To live a life for God involves loving Jesus and desiring his presence above all things and then pouring out love to the least and last, the lost and lonely, speaking for the voiceless, clothing the naked, feeding the hungry, declaring good news, and being good news to the world around—all from the overflow of time in his presence.

The fruit of these new insights was that God had gotten hold of me and broken my pride. When Daphne and I were approached again, we said we were prepared to consider coming. I met privately with the chair of trustees, and I explained my background, my past, my personal history and failure, and all the reasons why I didn't think I was the suitable person. The chair of trustees listened to it all and then asked if I was willing to allow her to pursue those stories and talk to some of the people involved. I said I was, but I clearly expected that those conversations would end the whole discussion.

In the meantime we visited again, expecting it to be for the last time. We set off and had driven only three miles when Daphne burst into tears and sobbed and sobbed. I was stunned and asked her what on earth was going on. She sobbed louder and told me that she had no idea. After half an hour of her further sobbing and denials of any known reason, I was frustrated and angry. It was only as we were arriving at Ffald-y-Brenin that she said it was homesickness, which presumably meant we were indeed moving there.

The Trust then contacted me and said that after their research they remained convinced I was the man for the job and that their desire to talk with me about the position was unanimous. We met, and they formally offered us the job. We felt that God had given us no choice, because at every point he had confirmed his call, so we agreed on the timing of our arrival and the strategy we would seek to implement. We were to develop a vision for the future. We would be residents on-site and supervise the wardens, who would undertake the day-to-day running of the place. The goal, however, was to build a new team and a new future for the center. It was expected that only a few hours a week would be spent in this role, but our presence at the center would provide the momentum for change.

We moved to Ffald-y-Brenin on the Saturday of the last week in October 1999. We had no money to get us there, as we had no income, but we were given sufficient funds to hire a truck and move ourselves. Our children came and joined us and helped us to pack the truck, and we set out on our 130-mile journey. It was a stormy night and a nightmare journey as I drove the vehicle with my son and son-in-law through the mountains in the dark, with leaves and debris everywhere and the windshield wipers fighting to function. We were also having issues with the vehicle's lights.

My eyes were tired from trying to see the road, and we were all feeling ragged, so we pulled into a lay-by for a break. We later discovered that we had driven over 120 miles and were only six miles from our destination! We had our refreshments, set out again, and drove into the valley. We became aware of lights moving high along the hillside, and after a while we realized they were ours. The weight in the back of the truck was causing the front to be lifted up so high that the lights were not shining on the road properly.

Finally we got to our new driveway—which is very steep. Halfway up, the clutch started to burn. Smoke rose from underneath the truck, and we started to roll backward. The brakes weren't holding, and it became clear that the truck wasn't going forward any farther. It was pouring rain when Daphne and our daughter (who had been following behind in the car) arrived and expressed both alarm and amusement at our plight. I reversed the truck down our steep driveway, warily avoiding the drop to one side. We then got in the car and drove up to the center and found some spare couches to sleep on that night.

The next day one of our new neighbors came around with a tractor and chain and towed us up the driveway. But our travail was not over yet, despite the warm welcome from the guests then in residence. The truck's rear tailgate was jammed by things that had fallen against it, and it was some while before we could pry it open.

I wasn't aware of it at the time, but I can see now that this was God reminding us that we came in helplessness. We couldn't eat, we had no income, we had no ability to live, and we couldn't actually even get up the driveway—we needed others to tow us in our helplessness.

As I pondered our new beginning in helplessness, I recalled the spiritual track down which I had come. I had first encountered church as a three-times-a-Sunday attender as a child. Our family moved to Oxford in the early fifties, and one night an illiterate lay preacher visited our church. My sister and I were fascinated by him. He recited his readings for the service and outlined the first verse of hymns from memory. On this particular Sunday I was touched by what he said and longed to get home to pray.

To my parents' surprise I went straight to my bedroom and knelt down. I prayed, "Lord Jesus, I want to live for you; I want to give my life to you. I want to be what you want me to be. I'll go anywhere you want me to go—my life belongs to you now." As a child I didn't realize the full importance of what I was saying. In many ways the rest of my life so far has been the story of my growth in understanding of what that meant, who it was I was speaking to, and what he's like.

I meant it though. I started preaching in a local Methodist circuit when I was fifteen. I later joined a Baptist church, where they seemed clear that I was being called into ministry. They encouraged me to get training, and I went to what was then called the Midlands Bible Training College to do their standard ministerial training course and a specialist course in evangelism.

As part of the course we took part in a mission at a Shropshire Baptist church. Local helpers included a schoolteacher called Daphne. We were soon friends, and romance blossomed into marriage before a year was out.

Our new life together was full of variety. Evangelism was the heartbeat of all I was doing, and I especially focused on Christian witness within the business community. When a new wave of the work of the Holy Spirit swept through the UK church in the late seventies and early eighties, we found ourselves immersed. People were eager to meet with God, and we poured ourselves into responding to their needs. There was a period of eighteen months when, apart from breakfasts, we never ate alone as a family. Our home was full of people seeking to follow Jesus. It was a wonderfully fruitful time. However, the next fifteen years were not easy, although there would be times of "wading in the water" again as the Holy Spirit touched the lives of many in 1994.

For all of us there are likely to be moments when God suddenly steps in and accelerates our steady progress toward maturity. One such incident happened to me during a holiday with relatives in

Lincolnshire when I was fifteen. My uncle, a Methodist lay preacher, mentioned that on Saturday morning he was going to a Christian bookshop in Grimsby on his Vespa scooter, and he invited me to join him for the ride.

As I waited for him to be served in the shop, I glanced round the bookshelves. My eye was drawn to a small hardback with a yellow dust jacket. It was as though it leaped out of the shelf at me, this glistening book shining like a beacon in a sea of gray. It was called *The Revival We Need* and was written by Oswald J. Smith. I'd never heard of him and had never read any Christian books except the Bible. I hovered for a moment but left the shop without the book.

That night I dreamed about the book, and I felt God saying that this was something I should read. I'd never experienced a prompting in a dream before and was unable to get the book out of my mind. A few weeks later I spied a Christian bookstall in the middle of a local market. There at the heart of the display was that very book, and within a few minutes I was reading words that would change the direction of my life.

In the pages of the book I was reintroduced to God. I discovered that he wanted more than Sundays and Bible reading. He wanted us to turn from sin and be clean, but he also beckoned us to come into his presence and commune with him. I found a God who listened to and responded to our prayers. I was taken to the Bible to discover the God who from creation had poured out mercy on his people and on nations who didn't know him and had poured out his Spirit of salvation on them.

For the very first time I was reading extracts from the stories of revivals in Wales and was stirred to a depth I could not understand.

I was seized and taken captive by the notion that it was possible to ask God to come and breathe upon people and change their hearts and win them. My goal was set. I wanted to be somebody who could say, "Father, will you come, and will you use me where I can be helpful? Will you come and rescue these people and bring them to a knowledge of you?"

And so there I was, nearly forty years later. Where could I be helpful? God had seemed to place us at Ffald-y-Brenin. It had been a hard first day, but surely it would get better. Not quite yet it seemed.

There were to be more surprises and more vulnerability. On our second Monday we met at nine o'clock for the first time with the warden and another trustee. I was about to open the meeting with prayer when I was interrupted by the warden, who asked if he could say something. He said, "We have covered this place since Peter died, and it's been a year almost to the week. It's been difficult. And now our daughter has given birth and there are difficulties, and we're desperate to be able to move and be near her. We're very sorry to spring this on you, but we're giving in our notice."

Within five minutes of starting our new task, everything had changed. Where would God take us now?

CHAPTER 5

LIVING IN THE PRESENCE

We were enjoying welcoming people who felt compelled to come up our driveway. But we began to feel that it would be good if the presence of the Lord touched people beyond the boundaries of our property. Very soon we had new people coming and knocking on our door. They were people who had been walking on the hillside on a path that brought them near our boundary or on a footpath that actually runs off the hillside and through the edge of Ffald-y-Brenin.

They often said the same first sentence: "Excuse me, but could you please tell us what's going on here?" Prompted as to why they were asking, they would say, "Well, something strange happened to us as we walked near your boundary," or, "Something came over us as we stepped onto the stile that took us from the hillside through your boundary." And in general what they would all say was, "We don't know what it is, but it's what we've always wanted."

One couple turned up who'd been struggling to come up the hillside near our boundary because they kept being knocked off their feet by what they described as an incredible and wonderful power such as they'd never ever experienced. It made them feel how they'd always wanted to feel all their lives, but they couldn't describe it. They couldn't put it into words, and they were reluctant to attribute it to God, as up to that point they hadn't believed in him.

Cups of tea are a key part of our ministry method, so we would chat to these puzzled visitors over a drink, give them a little walk around, take them to the chapel, and then either the Holy Spirit would fall on them, or we would just bless them and then the Holy Spirit would come and meet with them.

Our everyday guests began to encounter those being touched in this way. On the hillside near us, a path swings around following the contours of the land and comes close to our boundary by the high cross that we have erected. One day some guests were praying down there and noticed that the high ferns in the undergrowth were moving, despite there being no wind. They went over to investigate and to their surprise found a couple who looked to be in their thirties, on their backs, feet and hands in the air, tears pouring down their faces as they laughed and cried. Our guests retreated and continued praying but kept a wary eye on the ferns.

Soon they noticed the couple a little ways away, talking quite animatedly to each other. As they watched, the couple started walking back toward the ferns and suddenly fell down, laughing and weeping. After a while the overcome couple moved away and then noticed our watching guests. After an initial exchange of pleasantries, the couple explained what was happening to them: "When we walk on the path near the boundary, it's as though we're drunk and our legs won't hold us up, and we feel full of inexpressible joy. And we've found that if we get closer to the boundary it's stronger, but if we manage to crawl away it sort of lifts. Can you explain to us what's going on?"

The guests suggested that the couple come to the center and meet Daphne and me. With some difficulty they did, and in due course we met them and blessed them, and a process of faith discovery began for a couple who had been surprised by joy as they walked on a hillside.

For a season, as we continued to pray, people came face-to-face unexpectedly with God at the upper border of the property. Near a fence, on a hillside in an anonymous valley, they had their "burning bush" experience.

It would be tempting to think, as you read these Holy Spirit stories, that we live in a state of perpetual excitement. However, in reality we live lives that have plenty of room for both the mundane and the supernatural. A good way of explaining the work of the Spirit here is this: it's not a steady line; it's not an even incline. It's more like a wave that has ebbs and flows, and it is always in movement, either ebbing or flowing. There also seems to be seasons where there is a particular emphasis or type of work of the Spirit.

We recently had a particular season of the Spirit's outpouring that lasted about a year, which was notable for amazing inner healing. Scores upon scores of people visited who felt deeply broken by the realities of some aspect of their lives. Typically what would happen would be that God would wake them in the night and say to them, "Today is the time when I'm going to deliver you and heal you from the wounds of your past."

We've had other waves where people have come to faith, and we've had waves where people are spontaneously baptized in the Holy Spirit.

People leading healing retreats here have commented that they need smaller teams and that it's difficult not to be healed here. Alpha Holy Spirit events enjoy an ease of activity. When guests bring their not-yet-committed friends with them, these friends are often impacted by what they perceive to be a presence. Some fall down and are spontaneously converted and filled with the Holy Spirit. Some walk by the high cross and find healing coming upon them.

The "everyday Roy," if I can describe myself in that way, found the ebb times worrying. There would be fewer testimonies and the heavy sense of God's presence would seem to lift. I would be praying, "Oh God, search my heart, search my mind. Have I offended you, Lord? Is there a hidden sin here, Lord? Have you decided to lift your favor?"

The Lord spoke to me during one ebb in a very direct way. Some unexpected visitors arrived at our door. A local minister brought a visiting couple from the United States, the main teachers on prophecy for the whole worldwide Vineyard movement. The wife fixed an eye on me, and I suddenly knew that she'd gotten an important word from God for me. But I didn't know her, and I found myself juggling conflicting emotions. I was willing to hear from God, but I am wary of prophecies from strangers.

She just looked at me and said, "Can I share a word with you? God says that he works with you in ebbs and flows, and you get worried with the ebb. He is working in ebbs and flows with you so that his work is sustainable. And he allows the ebbs in order for you to consolidate and rest, take a deep breath, have time to rest and sleep, catch up on all the ordinary things that need to be done. This is so that you are able to sustain things during the next flow. This is God's plan and pattern of working with you." Whenever we're in a little bit of an ebb now, I remember that and trust God for something new and fresh.

One example of this relates to a church that comes here on a regular, seasonal basis to do their Alpha weekend. When they started, there were many signs and wonders. For quite a number of visits, the Holy Spirit was poured out on people and there were very visible manifestations. Recently, however, they've discovered that their weekends are quieter and there are no visible manifestations. That concerned me until they explained that there seemed to be a new depth of change emerging from those coming on the weekend. They said they would choose depth over manifestation.

So it seems that God gives periods of rest with these ebbs and flows, but we've also sought to guard ourselves from offending the Spirit by being partisan or sectarian. In a place like this there will always be visitors, people with good hearts and a desire to be part of what God is doing, who nevertheless want you to join in with their agenda.

One common area has to do with Israel. People will ask us to incorporate prayer for Israel. We agree, but only if they are happy to spend an equal amount of time praying for justice and peace for Palestinians too. This response can cause a great problem for some.

With others there'll be an issue, for instance homosexuality, that provokes a tirade. We have to intervene and let people know that we don't speak of homosexuals in that way. Homosexuals are made in the image of God, Jesus died for them, God's heart cries out for them, and we want to reflect him, so we want to cry out for them too. We don't shy away from believing that homosexual physical practice is outside God's purpose and as such is sinful. However, we are to love the people, and we bless them. We'll be praying and saying, "Lord, please come and touch and bless this person as much as anybody else." "Grace first" is our ethos.

We want to find a reason to bless everybody and everything, and there would have to be a very strong reason to do anything other than bless. And the truth is that the time God chose to send Jesus was the time when we were most lost in our sins: "For while we were still weak, at the right time Christ died for the ungodly" (Romans 5:6 ESV). We need to have the same attitude.

For some guests the center presents such a challenge to an underlying issue in their lives that they cannot stay. They realize that they can't escape from God here and so opt to leave. They arrive at our door an hour after they have been booked in and announce that they have to go. They tell us that God won't let them rest, but they are not ready to face up to the issues that are surfacing. They tell us, "I didn't know that his presence was going to be so up front and so inescapable." We bless them and pray that God will lead them into a place where they can respond positively to his call, but we see them go and are sad that they've been unable to respond.

It's been quite interesting with various tradesmen who have called here over the last few years. They have perhaps come to drop something off, but can't leave, and find themselves just standing and asking questions, sometimes hopping from foot to foot. They're so embarrassed. They are not sure what is happening to them but feel it's good. We get to share the blessing with them.

But not all of them welcome the presence of God. On one occasion a tradesman came to fix something at the center. After about ten minutes he came and told us that it was repaired and asked us to sign the form to say he'd been here. When I went to actually use the item he'd "repaired," I discovered it wasn't repaired at all.

The company sent somebody else out to repair it, and when he arrived, he couldn't understand what was going on, as no repair had been done. He called the other tradesman and was told that he had been overwhelmed with a fearsome sense of a presence that convicted him because of his way of life. So he lied when he said that he'd done the work. He was desperate just to get off the site; it was too frightening for him.

One of our regular speakers had an experience that initially worried her but was to become a landmark in our understanding of what God was doing here.

Jennifer Rees Larcombe leads retreats here and has been a great blessing to us. On the final morning of one weeklong retreat, she went to the meeting room that overlooks the valley to pray and ask God for any words that she should use to bless the retreat guests as they left for home.

As she prayed, she saw what looked like an angel sweep through the vaulted window and stand before her. She later explained that she was immediately clear that this was not a genuine angel because it wasn't taller than six feet, had wings with feathers, and looked like a child's Sunday school picture of an angel. As he stood before her, his wings shabby and some feathers missing, he looked extremely tired and worn. He leaned on a sword that had pieces missing from the blade. She cried out and asked God to deliver her from what she viewed as a demonic intruder.

But she felt the voice of God say that this messenger had been in battle on God's behalf and that his appearance spoke of the fierceness of the fight: "This is the messenger that I sent to fight for you in the heavenlies this week so that you would have the freedom to minister my love to my hurting children."

That just broke her heart open. She lost sight of the angel, but she stayed there, bowed on the floor, worshipping God. As she did, she heard the door behind her quietly open and close several times. When she could finally bear to get up, she turned and, to her surprise, lying on the floor were her team members. She didn't know what had brought them. It seemed that they'd been doing different things around the center, but the Holy Spirit had prompted each of them to go into the meeting room. As they opened the door and walked in, the power of the presence of God had taken each of them off their feet.

Jennifer explained what had happened with the angel and what God had said, and they all fell on the floor again and just worshipped. As they eventually began to stand up and speak to one another, they started to prophesy to each other. When they did, this power of God would come and take them off their feet again. This happened numerous times.

Jennifer decided that they had better return to the dining room and say good-bye to the guests before they left after breakfast. She opened her eyes but was overcome with a feeling that she had gone blind. Neither she nor the team members could see anything. After such an eventful time, was this another aspect of what God was doing in the situation? The answer was rather more mundane. It was late at night in our pitch-dark valley. They had been in the presence of God for over fourteen hours.

This significant visitation symbolically "drew back the curtain." It was as if God had said, "Let me show you what I'm doing for you in the heavenlies over this place that allows my mercy to flow."

There were more supernatural events to come. The following week a guest went into the chapel to pray. She thought she had been in there about ten minutes, but actually she was there several hours.

A short time later a group of pastors' wives came to stay. They wanted to network, get to know each other, and build relationships with each other, as they all came from the same locality.

On the first day, they planned to go out walking, so they got up, laid out their boots and socks ready for when they left after breakfast, and went down for the meal. As one of them started to say grace, the Holy Spirit fell on them, knocked them off their chairs, and onto the floor. They didn't get their breakfast, lunch, or supper. At around midnight, the weight of the presence of God began to lift off them. They were lost in awe and responded by worshipping. By now they were very tired, so they ate and drank and then went to bed.

The next morning they met up and agreed that they really would go for a walk this time. To be on the safe side, they didn't allow the person who had said grace the morning before to pray! They were a bit naughty really because they nominated someone they thought to be one of their more conservative sisters to pray. She prayed, "Father, we give you thanks," and the Holy Spirit rested on them and knocked them off their chairs again: no breakfast, no lunch, no supper. At about midnight the glory of God lifted off them and they decided to call their husbands to get them to come. Some were able to do so and they too had encounters with the God of grace.

A little while later we had a couple of women come to stay with us. One had been a widow for some years; the other was rather recently widowed. They were in the same church, but it was only because of the recent widowing experience that they had gotten to know each other. As they talked, it turned out that neither of them had had a vacation for years. They wanted to go together to somewhere that felt secure and safe, so they decided to come to Ffald-y-Brenin.

They stayed in the Hermitage, a small cottage overlooking the lawn and farmhouses. As they sat one teatime, the green at the heart of the center framed by the nearby window and the hills rising up in the background, the conversation turned to prayer and praying aloud. They marveled at the confidence of younger people who prayed in the meetings at church, but it became clear as they talked that neither of them had ever prayed aloud in public. They agreed together that they would like that freedom to pray, so they decided to have their own mini prayer meeting and pray a one-sentence prayer in front of each other. One of the women went up the steep steps to the bedroom, and they both spent twenty minutes crafting their short prayers. The walls in the Hermitage are eighteen inches to two feet thick. But before they prayed they opened the door and checked to make sure there was nobody nearby who could possibly hear them. They decided that after they prayed they would eat and then visit the local coastline, as it was about 5:15 and that would fill up their evening nicely.

The first read her prayer, and the presence of God touched them. The second read her prayer, and in their own words it was "just lovely." They were then thrown into some confusion when they opened their eyes to darkness and discovered it to be 3:00 a.m.

As far as they were concerned, God did something that day as they discovered a sense of his presence that they had not known before when they found the courage to pray to him aloud.

For a while people were a little wary of praying here if they had commitments later in the day. We had one couple of women who were going from here to a meeting, and God had done a work in them as they prayed. Now it seemed that they were going to be very late for their meeting, which was due to start minutes after they would be leaving the center. I prayed with them, and we asked the Lord to do something supernatural. They got into the car, and the driver was aware of starting the car, but the next thing they knew, they were at their destination six miles away, and they were there on time. It was physically impossible.

We've also seen some unusual phenomena in nature and with respect to a visible "glory." One Thursday we had our usual evening worship in the chapel. Unbeknown to us, an American friend, Dick, had arrived early for a meeting that was going on later in the evening. As he stepped onto our driveway he prayed, "Lord, I've heard of the stories of you doing many wonderful things at Ffald-y-Brenin. I've never seen anything like that, and I would really like to be able to say that I've seen something like that."

He couldn't find us at the house, so he wandered across the lawn and up the path to the chapel, thinking he'd have a time of quiet prayer. He discovered us there having just started our regular time of evening prayer and sat down on one of the benches against the wall. All of a sudden the weight of God's presence came, and we stopped and became quiet.

Then the presence grew and was almost overwhelming, and one of the guests burst into tears. It started getting very bright, and then brighter and brighter. I tried to look up but couldn't because of the brightness of the light. The chapel is round but the ceiling is like a cupola. And it was filled with an incredible and glorious light. Dick managed to squeeze out the words "It sure is getting bright in this chapel!"

For half an hour we sat in silence with this incredible light and the glory of God's presence. Eventually we rose and began to prepare for the meeting that I was now late for. As everyone gathered and we drank our cups of tea, Dick began to talk about what had just happened. As he did, the glory of God came again and rested on us, and for about an hour it was very difficult for anybody to speak or move or open their eyes.

Dusk had settled outside, but suddenly a rainbow appeared. It came straight in front of our window and went down into the valley and then turned and came straight across onto the lower land of Ffald-y-Brenin and stayed there. It had incredible and vivid colors. We gazed at it for quite a while—humanly it seemed completely unnatural.

The next morning my wife took a phone call from somebody across the valley asking whether she had seen the rainbow. Our neighbor seemed fairly clear that she had never seen a rainbow like that in her life and that it was God at work.

I don't put huge value on these astonishing events, and part of me is a little wary of even telling the stories. I think it's interesting that sometimes we see the worked-out, physical activities of God with people. It can encourage our faith, but our faith isn't in those things. We are seeking his face, not his manifestations. If manifestations come, we bless God; if they're not there, we don't worry for a moment. What we must have is his presence. We don't want people to be looking for manifestations. We just want them to look for Jesus.

Soon God would be prompting us that, for some, their healing would come as they looked to the cross, both literally and symbolically.

CHAPTER 6

THE BURDENS OF MY
HEART ROLLED AWAY

It was early 2004 when God placed another idea in our hearts about the things we were to do at Ffald-y-Brenin. One day, as I prayed, God gave me a vision of a cross that we were to erect on the land. The details were very clear and specific. There was a particular spot in the grounds where it should be placed, it was to be eight feet tall and four feet wide and was to face over the valley at a certain angle. We had a strong sense that this was very important. My nonconformist beliefs quickly swam to the surface and reminded me that it was only wood in a symbolic shape, but I felt it was a clear mandate from God, so I determined to go ahead.

In due course I met with our groundsman, and we went to the spot where the cross was to be placed. He was adamant it couldn't go there, as the ground was too rocky, and wandered off to find a place where there was enough topsoil to help anchor it. I dug my heels in and insisted it had to go where I suggested.

This provoked him to go and get some tools to prove to me the folly of my idea. He returned with a screwdriver and a very long blade. The hole needed to be as deep as the blade to support the cross. I tapped the spot with my foot and he thrust the screwdriver into what he thought was solid rock.

It plunged in up to the handle. His mouth literally fell open. He looked up at me and then he eased the screwdriver out. It brought out a solid cone of rock and we had a ready-made hole. We had a spare post-holder, so he went and found it and placed it in the hole, ready to be cemented in. We clarified the angle it was to be at, and soon we were ready for the next stage.

Over the hills from Ffald-y-Brenin was a wonderful shop. It's moved now, but it was like those stores you see in Wild West films where you can buy beans or bread but also get all the nails and wire and tools you need. I sent our groundsman there to get two pieces of treated outdoor timber. One had to be eight feet long, the other was to be four feet long. We also needed four nuts and bolts and washers to hold it all together

He returned looking pale and visibly trembling. I sat him down, and he explained what had happened. He had spoken to the shop owner, Gordon, and told him that he wanted some outdoor timber. Gordon was apologetic, saying that the normal delivery hadn't arrived and a local builder had taken just about every bit of wood in the place … except for a piece eight feet long and a four-foot-long remnant.

It was a day of small but significant miracles. I reassured my shaking groundsman that God was at work and it was okay.

The wood was treated, and a few days later it was ready to be placed in the ground. The groundsman got hold of the cross beam and hoisted it on his shoulders, and I went down and picked up the bottom end. He yelled at me to put it down, and I dropped it, fearing that it wasn't dry enough or something. He told me that he needed to carry it, but I could help him slot it into the holder. He felt somehow connected to the cross, so he carried it down the grassy path to the place where it was to be situated—two hundred yards away.

We placed it in position, and as he tightened the bolt, out of the corner of my eye I saw some movement on the main footpath off the hillside where it swoops down by our boundary. A woman had come over a ridge and suddenly seen the cross in front of her. She was rooted to the spot, and despite it being a cold late March day she was still there later as we packed up our tools and returned to the workshop.

I went down there an hour later, and the woman on the hillside path was in the same spot, staring at the cross. It began to dawn on me that the cross was going to be part of people's transformation, not merely a symbol on the hillside.

Not long after this, a group of women were here on retreat. Among them was a deeply troubled woman. She had no faith and had left her religious husband because of abuse. She found herself at the cross during her visit and experienced strong emotions of hatred because of what she had experienced in her life.

She walked up to the cross and spat on it and said, "God, I have never, ever believed in you, and if you were alive, I would spit on you because that's all you're worth. If you were real and you allowed me to go through the abuse I've been through, then you are no God that anybody should bother with." She spat on it again, and then she kicked it. She burst into tears and started hitting it, first with her hands and then with a piece of fallen wood from a nearby hedgerow. She was angry and declared, "If you were alive, you wouldn't be able to contain or handle my hatred, but you're not."

Eventually the anger, pain, and tears subsided, and she stood there sobbing. A voice spoke to her and said, "Take hold of the cross." She nearly jumped out of her skin, partly because she hadn't heard anybody come up behind her, but also because she thought she'd been careful to ensure that there was nobody around to see what she was doing. She turned, but there was nobody there. She was thinking that this was a little weird when she heard the same voice again. The third time she looked around again to check that no one could see her, and then, feeling rather foolish, she took hold of the cross. The same voice said to her, "Now move the cross." She was quite a substantial woman, but she couldn't move the cross at all. Then the voice said, "You cannot move it, because it's immovable. My love for you is immovable. I've been with you through your pain and through the abuse, and I hate what you've been through. I'm not for the abuse; I'm for you. I'm standing here so that you can pour out your anger, pain, hurt, and frustration onto me. I will carry it on the cross. My cross is immovable, just as my love is immovable. When you've poured all your anger and hatred on me, I will just say to you that I love you." Within moments she found herself weeping and kneeling in front of the cross, crying out a prayer of acceptance to a God she had never understood to be a God of love.

A few evenings later I was seated at the piano playing some worship songs in my front room. Some guests had wandered in, and we were just worshipping, but I was distracted by a strange movement at the edge of my vision. I turned and could see flames outside. I was worried that the hillside was on fire until a guest informed me that some of the women had taken items with occult symbolism at their heart down to the cross to burn them and offer a clean sacrifice to the Lord. The woman who had owned them was totally changed.

We then started finding that others were going down there and having substantial encounters with God. Sam had lost his wife to cancer. She had felt unwell, been diagnosed very quickly, and been told she had a year to live. She had died after six months. They were both firm believers, strong in their faith, and were in a very strong, supportive fellowship. After she died, the fellowship rallied around Sam and said, "We're standing with you and we're going to support you. We're going to be with you every step of the way." Several months later he came to Ffald-y-Brenin, and one morning he decided to walk down to the cross, since he'd never been there but he could see it from his window. He walked down there quite casually, but when he was about twenty yards away, he felt as though he had hit a brick wall. He couldn't walk any farther. His first reaction was anger with himself for not being able to get past this "invisible" wall. Eventually he turned around and went back. To his mind it was absolutely ridiculous that he couldn't walk up to a cross.

The next day he went down there again and the same thing happened. Somewhat nonplussed, he went and sat on a nearby stile and just gazed at the cross. Thinking out loud, he said, "Lord, what on earth is going on?"

He didn't expect a response, but he felt that he heard the voice of God saying, "Sam, I just want to touch the grief in your heart."

To his surprise he found tremendously deep sobs coming up from within him, and then he just wept and wept. Once again he heard God's voice saying, "I'm touching your heart and I'm setting you free from the depths of your grief. But now I want to touch the anger."

Suddenly he was aware of a powerful anger. Why had his wife been taken away? Why had it happened so quickly? What kind of God was it who would let this lovely Christian woman simply die from cancer? As the anger raged, he was aware of God's voice saying, "I'm touching your heart and I'm taking away your anger and I'm setting you free, but I want you to know that I have carried the pain of your wife and the pain of your grief."

The process continued for a while, and then he got up and simply walked straight to the cross and put his arms around it. Later he wrote to me and said that when he put his arms around the cross he felt his heavenly Father put his arms around him. He said it was like two people who hadn't seen each other for some time, hugging each other like old friends.

Sometimes groups of people gathered at the cross and God came to heal and reconcile. In the early summer of 2006 I was part of a group that was meeting here at Ffald-y-Brenin to look at difficulties and tensions between language groups in a nation. Part of the practical pastoral response involved people writing about the personal pain related to some of those conflicts.

The group leader had a small wooden eighteen-inch cross that she'd brought with her. We discussed the idea of people pinning their pain stories to this cross, but I suggested we might use our own high cross. A dozen or so of us made our way down toward it and, armed with a club hammer and six-inch nails, slowly nailed our pain to the cross. It was tremendously moving. After a while we took down the bits of paper, placed them in a bucket, and set fire to them. As the smoke rose, we praised and worshipped God for freedom and deliverance, the new identity that he gives us, and the new form of relationship found in his kingdom.

About a week later there was a knock at the door. A guest began to pour out her story: "Jesus woke me up in the early hours and told me that today's the day he's going to heal me and set me free. I don't really know what to do, but since six o'clock this morning I've been writing down the pain of the abuse that I've suffered." It was now eight thirty a.m.

I encouraged her to write down any remaining thoughts or memories, then when she returned two hours later, we said to her, "Why don't we take this paper down and nail it to the cross?" Daphne and I accompanied her but stood well back from the cross so that she could nail the thick wad of paper onto it with some privacy. When she had finished, she came and stood next to us. I then suggested she spend some time just looking at the paper nailed to the cross. She could remind herself that this was where all her past abuse and pain were now. This would help ensure that she would never forget; it would be imprinted on her mind that the past had been dealt with.

I asked her if there were abusive people she needed to forgive, reminding her that it is a costly thing to do. When we forgive those who have hurt us, we relinquish our right to vengeance. We are not saying that what they did doesn't matter anymore, and justice may still demand a response, but we are saying that it is now God's concern, not ours.

She acknowledged that God recognized how serious their sins against her had been, but she was going to let go of her anger toward these people and forgive them, believing that they were now account-able to God, not to her. So she forgave them, and we took the paper down. We then took it to a sheltered place, because it was windy, and set fire to it, giving thanks for freedom.

A few days later her minister called me and said, "I just want to tell you that the lady who's come back is the lady we have always thought might be lurking underneath the pain of this person, and we just want to say how wonderful the change in her is."

In the ensuing months many more would decide to take their brokenness to the high cross, hear God speaking to them, nail their pain to it, and see their healing begin.

As mentioned previously, Jen Rees Larcombe, the Christian author and speaker, leads retreats here most years. She felt that the placing of the cross in the ground actually did something to the land itself and changed the spiritual atmosphere. We didn't theologize about that, but we did think it was an interesting comment, because we too were aware that something had changed. Confirmation would arrive from an unexpected source.

A little while later we received a phone call from a woman who is a well-known pagan and occult leader in the area. She wanted to meet me, so we set a date, and I told the Lord later, "Well, Lord, all I'm really doing is being a passenger on this boat. I'm very interested in the ports that we call at, but you're the one who is setting the course. I'm following, and I'll just see what's going on here."

She came to Ffald-y-Brenin, and we gave her coffee, sat her down in the kitchen, and chatted a little bit. I asked her what she was up to at the moment. I felt sorry for her because she started to talk in detail about the occult stuff she was involved in. She couldn't stop herself from talking about it. She put her hand over her mouth at one point, trying to physically stop herself from spilling the beans about local occultism, but she could not stop it.

She told us how she related to angels and how angels directed her. According to her, these beautiful and wonderful angels actually didn't think much of Jesus at all and didn't like his agenda and had told her that their agenda was much better than his. I was fairly clear now on what we were dealing with but felt we should move the conversation forward. I asked why she wanted to see me.

She informed me that a new power had come into the area. It was so strong that it was nullifying all the work that she and others of her persuasion were trying to do. The same was true across the whole of Pembrokeshire. This was why she wanted to talk with us.

I asked what she knew about this stronger power, although I wasn't that interested in local occult power tussles! She looked at me as though I were a little bit dense and told me that our high cross was what had released the power that had nullified the occult activities of her and her friends. I thanked her for telling me, somewhat to her surprise, as she seemed to think I would have known. I asked her what she wanted. She said, "I want to bring a group of people with me to come and spend time at your high cross so that we can somehow harness that power and manipulate it."

To which I said, "Hmmmm—no!"

That was to be the end of the conversation for all intents and purposes. We do see her out and about in the community every now and then, and we do talk to her about the gospel. It's not something that she's open to at the moment, but one day, I believe, she will have ears to hear and she will turn. We pray for that day.

The placing of the high cross proved to be a spiritual catalyst for many, their "burning bush" experience, but it wasn't simply a good idea; it was a response to revelation. People come to Ffald-y-Brenin to ask me for the secrets that will provoke the presence of God. They want to know where to place their crosses. I have to tell them, as diplomatically as I can, that it's not like that. The key is searching for God, learning to listen for his voice, burrowing into his heart, listening to what he says, and then doing it, however simple or complex it might be. If he says it, do it. If he doesn't tell you to do anything, then why are you doing things? Why not just sit at his feet?

Some of the people who have gone down to the cross have literally sat at his feet. They've found themselves stuck to the ground. It has been an observable phenomenon that has shaken a number of people.

One person in particular, who didn't have a live Christian faith, went down and looked at the cross because he'd been told that he may well encounter God there. He didn't expect anything of the sort, so he wasn't disappointed when he first got there. But after sitting on the grass for a while, he found he couldn't take his eyes off the cross. He didn't quite know why, but there was something compelling about it. He was a young man in his thirties and was fit and strong, but when he decided to stand up, he could not push himself off the ground. He exerted all his muscle power but couldn't get up. Another guest walked down there and tried to get him up, but he was stuck.

The young man had been married recently, but to his alarm the moment he was married, he had discovered that his wife had a history of severe mental illness. He was so upset. He couldn't handle his wife, couldn't handle the pain, and couldn't handle the fact that her family had never told him of her history. Her illness was so severe that after a few weeks they'd split up. His doctor had advised him to come to Ffald-y-Brenin. So there he was, rooted to the ground, staring at the cross, but even with help he couldn't get off the ground.

After several hours he suddenly found he could move. As darkness fell, he felt compelled to go back to the cross, and he spent most of the evening there. Early the next morning he called his estranged wife and said, "I know you'll think this strange, but I'm at a place in Pembrokeshire called Ffald-y-Brenin. I really want you to come here."

At first she was very reluctant, but she soon relented and said she would come. I'm very grateful that neither Daphne nor I was there that day so we couldn't be involved or have a part to play. We prefer to let God do his thing and receive all the praise and glory.

Later in the day the man's wife arrived and he walked with her down to the high cross. They sat down and she turned and stared at the cross and then became ragged with sobbing and prolonged weeping. He didn't know what to do, so he just waited. After a while the deep sobbing and tears subsided and she began to explain how as a youngster she'd been abused and how she'd buried those experiences deep inside all her life. When it came to the honeymoon, her problems with sexuality came to the surface and she couldn't cope with it or the emotions or the marriage. No one knew of this abuse in her family circle. The couple talked a great deal there on the hillside and agreed that they would move back in together and commit to working through it together.

He wrote a note to us explaining all this and drew a picture of the cross with the comment "This is the surgery and it's always open."

For some it was heart surgery. But for many there would be a cure for physical illness and pain too.

CHAPTER 7

TOUCHING THE HEM
OF HIS GARMENT

Within the ebb and flow of life at the retreat center we began to see physical healing taking place for those among us who were sick.

One morning I popped over to collect a Bible that I'd left in the prayer room. On the way I saw a guest, a young woman in her late twenties or early thirties, coming down the steps toward the courtyard, holding on to the banister. She was coming down sideways, had no shoes on, and her feet were at a very funny angle.

My first instinct was to think that she had fallen and hurt herself, so I spoke to her to check that she was okay. She assured me she was fine and, noting my disbelief, she informed me that her posture was the result of an illness. She also told me that she didn't think God was going to heal her.

So I told her how thrilled I was to meet this unique person who had such an amazing and one-off relationship with God that he had given her a waiver with respect to all his normal promises. I think she was a bit thrown by that, but she agreed to sit and tell me what was going on in her life.

By the time she was twenty she was riddled with chronic osteo-arthritis. Despite this she managed to go to college, and during her time there she became a Christian. Her fellow students were keen to pray for her healing, especially given that by now she was in a wheelchair most of the time. Their prayers and those of some well-known ministers didn't usher in her healing, and she had decided that God wasn't going to heal her.

I shared a little bit with her about my understanding of healing and my own experience of God healing me. Following a car crash, I was in the operating room of a casualty department where the surgeon asked me to sign a consent form for the amputation of my left foot. I declined and trusted God, having heard his voice. I still have the same foot and enjoy plenty of exercise to this day. You can hear the full account of these amazing events in my audio recording titled *A Great Deliverance*.

This young woman was now thirty-two, and surgery had given her new hips and knees. She was hoping for future elbow and shoulder replacements and was about to go to the hospital for the first ankle replacement.

I asked if I could pray for her ankle. She was somewhat less than full of faith and said, "Well, I suppose if you must, you must." I knelt down and placed my hand on her ankle. I might as well have put my hand on a piece of dead wood for all the life that was there. I started to pray healing for her ankle, but it was clear there was nothing going on at all, and she certainly had no faith for anything.

I then started blessing her ankle, quite loudly, to disguise what I was saying inside, which was, *Oh God, deliver this poor young woman from my praying, my interference, and don't let this in any way push her into cynicism, but, Lord, do something about faith for her.* Suddenly I sensed God saying, "I've planted a seed of faith in her, and it's going to grow."

I was a little doubtful. Because of the situation I wasn't really quite 100 percent sure whether this was really God or whether this was me creating an out because the healing wasn't happening. I prayed quietly about it while I was still loudly blessing her ankle. I decided to tell her that God had put a seed of faith in her and that it was going to grow. She thanked me and then joined her mother-in-law, who had parked the car at the bottom of the steps and was waiting to take her home.

Apparently her ankle got worse and worse over the next few days. She became indignant about this, and she told God she didn't want to put up with it and asked him to do something. She was encouraged when it returned to the condition it had been in when I had prayed for her.

The day came for her to visit the doctor. Her husband wheeled her through the hospital straight down to the specialist's office. He was waiting, and the X-rays were lit up on the wall. They listened as he explained the operation process. All of a sudden she felt as though everything she was seeing was beginning to fade away, and she heard my voice speaking to her: "God is putting a seed of faith in you which will grow." Suddenly she felt something in her chest, which grew and grew until she felt as if she could hardly breathe.

She interrupted the specialist midsentence: "Excuse me. I'm sorry to interrupt, but I don't believe I need this operation at all. I believe God has healed me." Her husband, who had just wheeled her in, panicked and thought, *It's gotten to her brain. She can barely walk and even then she has to hang on to something.*

The specialist said, "Well, that's very, very interesting. What I'd like you to do is to take your shoes off, get out of the wheelchair, and walk around the office." She had been unable to do this for years. She bent down to undo her shoes, and as she took off each shoe, she felt something grow and burst inside her. She eased herself out of the wheelchair, and when she began to put weight on her feet, for the first time in years, her feet moved into the normal position on her legs till they were at right angles.

Very slowly at first, and then faster, she began to walk around the office. Then she began to run around the office, and then she started to laugh, and then she began crying at the same time. Her husband's mouth was wide open as he watched her.

The specialist said that he would need to do proper clinical tests, so she was taken for more X-rays and tests. Later in the day the young woman and her husband reported back to him. The specialist told her that she was a very perceptive woman and that, as there was nothing wrong with her ankles at all, she wouldn't need an operation.

Some months later I heard talking in our kitchen and popped in while on the way to fetch something. Gathered around the table were a couple with a very young child. The woman jumped up and said, "I'm so pleased to see you. Do you recognize me?"

I didn't recognize her. She explained who she was, and there she was, standing normally, talking to me quite animatedly about her story. When they left, we had the joy of watching them get up and walk down the driveway like any other couple would.

As the healing presence of God started to become apparent, we spent time in the chapel blessing what God was doing and blessing him for it. It wasn't very long before we started seeing more happening. It didn't happen because we held healing meetings—it seemed to just happen in the everyday circumstances of life at the center or in the context of our usual meetings.

Some weeks we can be full with individual visitors. When that happens, we sometimes encourage everyone to gather in the chapel on a midweek evening. We lay out the prayer room in a circle, and we have a candle that we light as a symbol of God's presence. In the middle of the room we have some kneeling cushions, some very substantial floor cushions, and a chair for anybody who would find it physically difficult to kneel on cushions.

We have a time of quiet, followed by some set, straightforward prayers that honor Jesus as Lord and some brief Scripture readings. I'll speak for maybe fifteen minutes about receiving mercy from God, then we say the Lord's Prayer together. After that, we invite anybody who would like to receive from God to come and kneel. When they come forward, somebody will put a pashmina over each of their heads to symbolize the fact that we are covered in the righteousness of Jesus, which means that whoever they are or whatever they've done, they can receive from God. This also echoes the idea of the robe of righteousness symbolism found in Isaiah 61:10.

We anoint their foreheads with oil, and we bless them in the name of the Father and the Son and the Holy Spirit. That's all we do. We don't ask them why they're responding; we don't pray for them.

I explain that they can stay there as long as they like and receive from God in simple and childlike ways. We encourage them to speak quietly to God and lay before him what they need or may be desperate for.

When everyone who wants to has been anointed, we will perhaps turn on some quiet music in the background. Typically many remain for some time, unable to move because of the weight of God's glory.

It's not always quiet and reflective though. One evening Suzie responded. As far as we knew, she was not a committed Christian. She had barely knelt before she gave a cry and landed flat on the floor and began to weep like an inconsolable baby. It was clear she was going to be some time, so we blessed her and moved on to praying for others. She was still weeping loudly when we had finished. By this time I was extremely tired, so I just blessed her again and left her to it.

The next morning we had our chapel time, but our weeping woman, who had not missed a morning meeting previously, was not there. It crossed my mind that the previous night might not have been a good experience for her, but one of the other guests talked to me after chapel and a different story emerged. The other guests had been having disturbed sleep all week because Suzie had been pacing her room and walking up and down the corridors at night. She had a serious sleep disorder and was terrified of sleeping because of the things that came to her when she slept. She could sleep only when exhausted, and even that sleep would be disturbed by nightmares.

Some time after I'd left the meeting the previous evening, the crying stopped and she started to laugh. (Some ministry, huh?) Some guests lingered to keep an eye on her. She laughed for exactly the same amount of time that she'd cried. Afterward, they helped her back to her room, where she collapsed onto the bed. They didn't hear anything all night, and she didn't appear in the morning, so someone nudged the door and looked in to make sure she was all right. She was exactly where she'd fallen the night before, absolutely sound asleep, undisturbed, totally set free of the things that had troubled her.

Sometimes the healing was a response to recent injury. One night Daphne and I returned from indulging in the small luxury of fish and chips from over the mountain only to be greeted by an anxious woman. One of our guests had tripped and fallen, damaging her hand very badly, and was on the telephone to NHS Direct (a health-information service) even as we spoke. I was assured that all was under control, but I insisted on seeing the woman. We needed to be clear about what had happened and how it was being handled.

I found the woman with the phone in one hand and a towel round the injured arm, which was being supported by a friend. The friend lifted the towel to reveal a horrendous injury. She had tripped on the hem of her long skirt and fallen sideways onto one hand and separated the fingers. The hand and arm were black, and there was no sign of a wrist—just a swollen expanse from the ridge of her knuckles to her elbow.

As she continued the phone call, I whispered, "May I pray?" She nodded, and I commanded the swelling to go down by half and to do so safely. During the next twenty to thirty seconds the swelling went down by half. I commanded the blackness to go and that took about a minute; then I commanded the rest of the swelling to safely disperse, and that took about forty-five seconds. It was all back to normal shape, except for the ridge by the knuckles on the back of her hand, so I commanded that to safely disperse, and it did. She couldn't move her fingers, however, so then I commanded a loosening of the fingers, the joints, the tissue, and the muscle and a cessation of the pain. Suddenly she could move her fingers comfortably and easily with no difficulty.

Now came the difficult part: How was she going to explain this to the health official on the phone? She said, "I'm ever so sorry, but I'm actually calling you from a Christian center, and as we've been talking, somebody has just prayed for me. I'm now healed, and I don't need any help at all."

She suddenly pulled the receiver away from her ear, and I could hear a torrent of abuse coming from the telephone for wasting the health official's time. She quietly put the phone down and rejoined the other guests, who were absolutely overjoyed and thrilled to have witnessed this remarkable healing.

God healed another accident victim early one morning: a United Reformed Church minister who had tripped and twisted her ankle. Her husband came to let us know he was taking her to the hospital. We took a chair, and she hopped toward the car, resting on the chair every so often. We got her into the main lobby, where she rested while her husband brought the car closer. I asked if I could look at the ankle. It was massively swollen, and she couldn't move her toes.

She suggested I pray. I commanded half the swelling to disperse safely, and it speedily did. Then I commanded the foot to go back to its proper position, and it did, and we spoke healing into the ligaments. I then prayed that the pain might go. She said it greatly diminished and affirmed that following more prayer she had regained full movement in her toes.

Her husband drove her to the hospital to have what I believed to be a bad sprain, which was already healing, treated. Three hours later they called us to say that her ankle was broken, the hospital had put it in a cast, and they were now off for a picnic.

Later in the week they joined us for a meal and brought us up-to-date. To be honest, I was quite agitated. To my way of thinking it was not in God's plan that she had a broken ankle.

As she sat down in our farmhouse kitchen, I looked at her big heavy cast, and it glared back at me accusingly. I asked if we had prayed at all about her bones or only for the tissue. Her answer was very clear: "No, you didn't pray for the bones, and I'm quite cross about that. Would you mind doing so now, because I want to get rid of the cast?"

Her husband counseled common sense, but she insisted on prayer then and there. So I spoke to the bones and commanded them to be healed in the name of Jesus, and I also prayed for the whole healing process to be telescoped. She was full of faith, said "Amen," and indicated that she would be glad to be rid of the cast the following week. Her worried husband advised her to be cautious.

They stayed at the center longer than planned, as they needed to go back to the local hospital for a checkup. The hospital was not happy with the X-rays, but she asked them to remove the cast. After some resistance, they agreed and gave her a lighter cast.

They returned home and settled back into their routine, although she was still not very mobile. After a few days she was alone in the house one day and the moment she got up and started walking around, she had dreadful pains in her lower leg inside the cast. The local health center wasn't open, so she called NHS Direct, who said that it sounded like a blood clot and to get to Accident and Emergency right away.

The hospital staff acted fast and cut off the cast. As soon as they did so, the pain disappeared completely. It was thought best for her to have an X-ray, but the results were perplexing, so they asked her to wait and see a specialist. The specialist asked her if she could explain why she had a cast when there was no break apparent and there was no evidence of any previous break whatsoever. He was concerned that someone had given her an unnecessary cast.

So she gave thanks, and nursing a slightly stiff, bruised ankle, she returned to normal life, all the while thanking God for his grace and blessing.

We rejoice when people who are sick and injured are healed. It's wonderful. These signs of the kingdom, expressions of God's mercy, are deeply encouraging. At the end of the day, though, we're all going to decay and die. Lazarus was raised from the dead by Jesus, but in due course he still died. The issues of life and death are in God's hands, and death is ultimate healing. We ask God to bring inner healing to people so that the internal limp that some have is healed, as well as the external illnesses that others suffer from.

We have learned to find precious the words of the prophet in Isaiah 53 about the future sufferings of Jesus:

> Who hath believed our report? and to whom is the arm of the LORD revealed? For he shall grow up before him as a tender plant, and as a root out of a dry ground: he hath no form nor comeliness; and when we shall see him, there is no beauty that

we should desire him. He is despised and rejected
of men; a man of sorrows, and acquainted with
grief: and we hid as it were our faces from him; he
was despised, and we esteemed him not. Surely he
hath borne our griefs, and carried our sorrows: yet
we did esteem him stricken, smitten of God, and
afflicted. (vv. 1–4 KJV)

He bore not only our sins but also our griefs and our pains as he
hung on the cross. He carried our griefs so that our healing might
be one that touches the whole person. We've discovered that God
simply draws broken people here to Ffald-y-Brenin so that they can
discover more about the one who will get to the root of their pain.

They're not always the people you would expect to be inwardly
broken, because many of them are boisterous about their faith and
clear in their testimony. But when they've been here a little while,
you find them cracking open. The truth comes out, because the Holy
Spirit is touching them. It's a safe place, and surgery can take place
here. It's spiritually clean; it's safe for surgery.

It often involves dreams. It's so supernatural, and the testimony
of people who are set free is wonderful. For many, their breakthroughs
come at the high cross, but the chapel has also been a "thin place" for
some, somewhere our separation from the heavenly realms seems to
become far less. We sometimes encourage people to take to the cross
small stones that signify the pain, the abuse, the hurt, and the brokenness. They lay them before the cross and speak out: "Lord, I let
go of these now. I'm giving them to you, and I declare in Jesus' name
that I'm free of them. They're not going to reign over me anymore."

It seems clear to me that it's impossible biblically to separate the good news of the kingdom from healing, because if you actually read the account of the Gospels and Acts, they flow together, so that when mercy flows out to us it is not just to help us find forgiveness for sin, but it's also to do with all that we are. This unstoppable stream, this river, this flood that is released upon us touches every part of our lives.

God's first instinct is to act with compassion toward us. He doesn't limit that compassion simply to our spiritual welfare, but extends it to every part of us. So if we are body, soul, and spirit, then his compassion reaches out into those three areas and loosens blessing. So where the presence of God is, there is healing.

When Jesus came into a community, it was good news for those who were open to welcome him. Although they were amazed by his words and teaching and dazzled by the miracles, it was the overflow of his life that was such good news for them. He didn't walk in, find a box in the village square, and start to preach, then make a speedy departure afterward. He reached out to the sick and healed them, opened blind eyes, restored deaf ears, lifted the weight of condemnation off the guilty, and prompted them to live a different way in the future.

All this, he taught, was a sign that the kingdom of God had come upon them. His healing miracles were not an incidental happening while he got on with the real business of preaching the gospel. He was the gospel. It was the overflow of his presence empowered by the Holy Spirit that was the breaking in of the kingdom.

When Jesus commissioned the disciples, it was with the instruction to mirror his own ministry. They were to heal the sick, release the oppressed, and declare that the kingdom of God was close. God cares for the whole person, and the gospel, the good news, is for the whole person. We have sometimes narrowed the gospel to a clear theological definition of sin and forgiveness, thereby robbing it of its breadth, power, and life. Today, around the world, God is stirring his people up to recover the gospel of Jesus, which is the gospel of the kingdom, and we want to be among those who will obey his injunction and seek the kingdom before all else. (You can hear more about the gospel of the kingdom in my audio recording titled *Your Gospel Is Too Small.*)

Sometimes the presence is simply enough—as we began to discover. We'd been very busy, and Daphne and I hadn't had time to see each other very much. One sunny day we agreed to meet on the lawn for tea at three o'clock and guard that time so we could have thirty minutes to catch up and enjoy each other's company.

We'd been there only a few minutes when a guest spotted us. As she made a beeline for us, we murmured "Oh no" and didn't begin to make welcoming moves or sounds. Despite our rudeness, she asked if she could share what God had done for her. My outer politeness in response masked my inner thoughts. She had arrived only a few hours before, so we had to consider bracing ourselves for her life story, according to my line of reasoning.

She had been shown to her room but had made checking out the chapel a priority. She had sat down quite rapidly and said she felt as if she had been submerged in the presence of God: "I couldn't move and I didn't want to. I just soaked in his presence; it was amazing."

After about an hour the weight of it had lifted from her, and she went to make herself a drink in the guest common room. She made fruit tea because of her long-term intolerance to other ingredients. But then it occurred to her that having spent time immersed in the presence of God, maybe the "rubbish" she had carried into the room was gone. So she made herself a normal cup of tea with milk and then in faith sipped it. Normally she'd only have to sip something with milk in it and there'd be a violent reaction. There was no reaction. So she took a mouthful: again, no reaction. She drank all of it, found a mug and a pan, and made herself a mug of milky coffee. She drank all of it as well. No problem.

She was on a roll now and decided to check what had happened with her wheat allergy. She had not eaten bread for eight years. She made herself a sandwich and ate it—there was no reaction. She had been set free.

Over the following weeks I shared her testimony with others, and they were spontaneously delivered of the same allergies.

Healing simply flows from the presence of God, but often we don't receive it because we're unaware that it's there to be received. Kathryn Kuhlman, a healing evangelist in the sixties, wrote about this type of healing in the presence of God. I read her books several times as a student but concluded that she was a woman of her time in a particular culture, with a framework of thought, religious language, and strong emotions that didn't connect with me. I did sense, however, that it was so clearly God. It spoke to me of what God is like and of what good news his caring and compassionate character is.

This healing in his presence didn't always happen in the most straightforward of circumstances. A group from a London church with ethnic roots came to stay. On their first evening the pastor was very keen that I share about the center and what God was doing here after their meal. But their car had broken down on the way, and they were eating very late—nearly 10:00 p.m. I tried to persuade him to wait until the next day, but he would have none of it.

When I got there at the agreed time, they were still eating. Fifteen minutes later they were still eating. Another fifteen minutes would pass before I got up to speak. After a few stories about how God was at work at Ffald-y-Brenin, I suggested that they might be tired. They kept asking for more until I declared that I was too tired, even if they weren't.

The pastor then asked if I would just listen to a story they wanted to tell me. He pointed out a short, white-haired, dark-skinned man who looked to be in his eighties. He had been with the pastor some months before when they had visited the center on a planning trip. They had gotten lost on the way and could stay only five minutes, because they had to return for another meeting. We talked, and they told us that they had been longing to find such a place. It was going to be the "prayer mountain" for their church in London.

Then they literally ran back to the car. They had taken the path from the house to the car park via the side of the chapel. The elderly man paused while the pastor began to get the car ready. He opened the chapel door and stuck his head inside. He pulled his head back out, closed the door, and went up to the car.

By the time he reached the car, his swollen arthritic joints weren't swollen anymore. He got into the car and moved very slowly and carefully as he fastened his seat belt because of the acutely painful frozen shoulder that he'd been having treatment for over the past two years. Suddenly it dawned on him that it wasn't frozen or painful at all.

He felt as though he had "stuck his head into God's heart." He was full of joy for several days but then started to become unwell. It took the doctor a while to get to the root of the problem. He was taking a large dose of medication for extremely high blood pressure. Because of what God had done, he didn't have high blood pressure anymore, so the tablets were reducing his blood pressure too low.

I love this sort of thing. To me it is just so God, so openhearted.

All of this unscripted healing was a challenge to our traditional methods, picked up over many years of church life. Our habitual response to personal need was to open up counseling conversations, where we responded to people's stories with appropriate scriptural verses and prayer.

It could be a very lengthy process. With a captive audience, people feel free to share every detail. There was fruit from this approach, however. We had laid hands on people and built the word of God into them and seen many miracles, but you could see only a few people per day and you quickly became emotionally drained.

On our journey of discovery about being a house of prayer, we were immersing ourselves in Scripture and started thinking again about the gospel of the kingdom. It reminded us that the kingdom of God often seemed to be very small in our thinking. Our God was great but the scope of the good news we shared seemed narrow. We were good on the moment of salvation, but perhaps weak on the salvation life.

The compassion of God does not cease toward us once we have committed our lives to him. This Father is not just for Christmas; he's for ever and ever. His compassion never fails. He is the same yesterday, today, and forever. If we long to see the sick, injured, or troubled healed, it is a reflection of our Father's heart moving through us.

Our guests are not usually with us for very long, so we don't always get to know them that well. But God knows every intricate detail of their situation before they even open their mouths. It wasn't illogical that he might therefore be dealing with people here with very little intervention from us.

We began to move away from the old prayer and counseling framework as our default model. It seemed to us that we should simply ask people, "Are you willing for God to come and touch this area of your life that is troubling you?" If they are, we pray for a moment, and I ask God for any specific word of knowledge or discernment or prophecy that he wants to apply to the situation.

Sometimes he gives us something, and sometimes he doesn't. When he does, it tends to be one simple, straight-to-the-point sentence. It goes directly to the bull's-eye and takes the wisdom of God immediately to the heart of the issue. We invite the person to turn to God and deal with God—who is now interacting with them. We turn them away from us so they cannot even physically see us, and we walk away and encourage them to continue to interact with God. The Holy Spirit is faithful to bring to a good conclusion what has started in that moment.

A good example of this was one experience we had fairly early on in our time at Ffald-y-Brenin. We were finding the behavior of one male guest somewhat bizarre, especially in our chapel times. I talked to Daphne, and we were very clear that helping him was a job for his local church and that we would not engage with him regarding his spiritual need.

One morning Daphne led chapel, as I had to be elsewhere. On my return she told me that she had promised him that we would pray with him. I was not happy and was threatening not to pray with him, but Daphne persuaded me, and I relented, as long as it was clear we would not be counseling him.

So, with my occasional Mr. Grumpy mind-set firmly in place, I went to the room where we were to meet. I sat down and inquired how he was. He just looked at me, and his eyes filled with tears. He said, "I am so unhappy." As he said it, it was as though an arrow had gone into my heart, and my own eyes filled with tears too.

He was happily married but hadn't been able to smile or laugh for two years. I asked him if he could identify any cause of such deep unhappiness, and he started to list about a thousand root causes. I stopped him and emphasized that I didn't need to know, as God already knew all the details of the situation. Then I started to pray: "Lord, come and help us," and I addressed the man with "Friend, I bless you in the name of Jesus. I bless you with the anointing of the Holy Spirit." The Spirit prompted me with a sentence, and I shared with the man what God had suggested was the real issue.

It was like taking an axe to a log and splitting it. It opened him up to the core. All the defenses were gone, and he just wept. When that had subsided a little, I looked at the various mats that were on the nearby table and encouraged him to pick up a coaster for each of the major things that were involved in this issue. I told him we should go to the chapel, where he could decide whether he was willing to lay those pains down at the foot of the cross and let God carry them instead. I expected him to take one or two of the coasters, but he counted them, looked around, and then scooped up all of the coasters in the room. His list would have been endless if I had allowed him to carry on.

He took one step toward the chapel and fell headlong on the floor, crying like a baby. His wife was upset, and he was rather embarrassed, but it was actually quite moving. We made slow progress as he continued to weep and stumble toward the chapel. Eventually we got to the cross in the chapel, and he quietly prayed there and laid those things down.

We then sent him off to the high cross with a comfortable outdoor cushion and told him to talk to God alone. Thirty minutes later his wife came to us, concerned that he had not returned. They were on a schedule and needed to leave. Another hour passed, and we suggested she go down there and check that all was well.

She came scurrying back up the path, saying, "I think I'm going to need your help. He has the appearance of being paralytic drunk. He cannot stand, he just falls everywhere, and he can't stop laughing." We went to her aid and got him in the car.

In Luke's account of the Day of Pentecost found in Acts 2, we read of Peter saying to the crowds, "These men are not drunk, as you suppose" (v. 15). When the Holy Spirit falls on people, they can act as though they are inebriated. It's not the way I would do it, but God is God, and it's the way he often moves. And who in their right mind would object to being thoroughly immersed in love, joy, and peace?

CHAPTER 8

THAT VERY OLD TIME RELIGION

It may sound like nonsense, but I think it's possible to be very clear about what God is doing and slightly confused at the same time. I know I have driven Daphne and some of my friends a little crazy quite often during the grace outpouring that we have experienced here.

The tension was this. I was observing all the things that God was doing, blessing them and loving them. But I was also asking how I could connect it all together and express it in words. I like to take a global view of things and see how things fit together for the big picture.

During that time if somebody asked me what was going on at Ffald-y-Brenin, I would struggle for ages, not knowing quite how to respond. I couldn't find a shorthand description that made sense of all that was going on that satisfied me, let alone anyone else. I was supposed to be managing the center and fostering new direction, but I couldn't quite articulate the vision.

A few years earlier I'd begun to look at some of the information that was emerging around the UK about the early Celtic Christians in our nations. The oft-repeated story about Augustine bringing Christianity to these islands is by no means the truth. There was a strong, vibrant, and organized church hundreds of years before the Augustine mission. The impetus for this came from the Celts. Here in west Wales we're surrounded by Celtic monuments and stories; it's the most densely populated area in the UK with respect to Celtic remains.

I soon learned a great deal more about the history of Christianity here in Pembrokeshire. In the early sixth century an Irish Christian called Brynach arrived at Milford Haven, and local pagan people began to be won to the faith. He planted another community in Haverfordwest before moving into the Gwaun valley here below Ffald-y-Brenin. He asked the small community that lived by the river whether he might have a piece of land and live among them. He didn't have an easy time because of the witchcraft and paganism that was part of life in the valley.

Fifteen hundred years ago, Brynach used to climb the hill on which Ffald-y-Brenin sits to the rocks on the top, from where he would intercede for the area. His depth of prayer and intercession seems to have been remarkable, and the local people became aware that the hillside was a "holy place." It was believed that as he prayed, angels came to strengthen him, and there were manifestations of God's presence with him on the hillside. The hill became known as Carn Ingli—the hill of angels. We are inheritors of remarkable spiritual history at Ffald-y-Brenin.

As I talked to people about Wales, revival, and the presence of God, I became aware of a specifically Welsh sense of connectedness to the land. Whenever God acts in Wales, somehow the land is involved. Today there are many people right across Wales who talk very seriously and quite profoundly of the last national revival in 1904–1905. There have been other moves of God, powerful moves of God and revival, in localities within Wales since then, but it is felt that the revival in 1904–1905 was stopped before it had run its course and that there is somehow a song to God still buried in the land, waiting for release. What does this mean?

If I am sure no one can hear me, I occasionally sing in the bath. There is one particular note that fills the room and sounds fuller and stronger than any other, almost as though the room itself has joined in the song. That's what happens in Wales. It is easy to praise God in Wales, particularly when we worship in Welsh. It feels as though there is a reverberation of something deep within the land that joins in, almost as though the worship has released creation and set it free to participate.

The psalmist seems to have understood this dynamic when he wrote, "Make a joyful noise to the LORD, all the earth; break forth into joyous song and sing praises! … Let the sea roar, and all that fills it; the world and those who dwell in it! Let the rivers clap their hands; let the hills sing for joy together" (Psalm 98:4, 7–8 ESV).

During a cold and stormy afternoon on January 15, 1905, hundreds of people gathered at the mouth of our river to witness ninety-two folks being baptized in the chilly waters. A witness wrote poetically of how "the rocks and spray joined in the praise."

To eyes that can see, it is as if there is something of God's purpose that's actually held and stored within the land. Because of the nature of the land here in Wales, the lyrics of our praise and worship songs resonate very strongly. There are hills to be climbed, there are plains to be crossed, there are rivers to be forded to a new and better place. So the land speaks loudly to us of the nature of God, of his creative and loving power in our midst.

As you move out from the hill and valleys around Ffald-y-Brenin, you discover a rich spiritual heritage. Thirty miles away is the cathedral of St. David, the patron saint of Wales, who traveled and preached across the land. His close friend Justinian established a missional monastic order that spread throughout Wales from this area. Farther along on the south coast was the remarkable Celtic settlement of Illtud, thought to be the cleverest and most brilliant man of his generation. He established a monastic community with 24–7 prayer at its heart lasting for years. It included a hospital and a university and had over a thousand people in the community at some points in its history. It seems that the area breathes mission.

We also found that it seems to breathe out revival. David Morgan, who was the pioneer of revival in 1859, came from nearby Cardigan. This period of time also saw historical revivals in Scotland and Northern Ireland. In Wales alone one hundred thousand people came to the Lord in a very short span of time, a significant figure given the small population of Wales then. At Blaenannerch, a village a short distance up the coast, David Morgan visited one evening in January 1859, and six weeks later the little Baptist chapel had welcomed twenty-eight young people, and another sixty people had been converted.

In 1904, in the same chapel, a young man and student in his twenties, Evan Roberts, was remarkably filled with the Holy Spirit.

There were already stirrings of revival in Wales at this time, but it deepened and spread after Evan went back to the chapel that had sent him out as a student. He had had to dig in initially to see any movement among the young people of his chapel, but their breakthrough would prove to be a catalyst for the Welsh revival of 1904–1905, which in turn would be part of a worldwide move of the Holy Spirit that continues more than one hundred years later. We're rooted and surrounded by all this glorious testimony of God's faithfulness and mercy.

All of this history provoked my curiosity, and I started to explore how the early Celtic Christians lived and how they viewed creation as the fifth gospel and how it communicated something about God.

We have the record of an old Welsh poem, written around the ninth century:

> Almighty Creator, it is you who have made the land
> and the sea.
> The world cannot comprehend in song bright and
> melodious,
> Even though the grass and the trees should sing,
> All your wonder, O true Lord!
> The Father created the world by a miracle;
> It is difficult to express its measure.

The Celtic Christians established their monasteries, but they seemed different from the withdrawn communities of some sections of the Latin church. Here was a form of monasticism that was community based and reflected the local people. It welcomed singles, it welcomed the young, the old, married couples, celibates, babies, and children—all were welcome within the monastic community.

At the center of each community was a rhythm of worship and prayer. They were constantly reminded of the foundation they stood on in the character of God, the work of Christ, and the empowerment of the Holy Spirit. They seemed enfolded and enthralled by the idea of the kingdom of God and the teaching of the Sermon on the Mount (Matthew 5–7). They had physical boundaries to their communities, but these tended to be merely practical aids to keep the chickens in. They were open to the community, and people visited and left in a fairly informal way.

I began to see a pattern that was very relevant to our sense of living in the presence of God at Ffald-y-Brenin. The Celts claimed the land for the sake of the kingdom. They established practices that encouraged prayer and worship and good relationships, but from which service, grace, mercy, education, healing, practical help, and mission poured out. Here was the place of mercy, acceptance, health care, education, and mission. Literally thousands of Celtic Christians poured out from these isles into Europe to win many to Christ.

The more I read, the greater my sense of "connecting the dots" became. I next looked at their use of liturgy. The firm but gentle repetitions of the liturgy enabled even the child or the illiterate to grasp the key traditions of the gospel, to participate in the prayers, and to learn the Scriptures as they worshipped. Their heart was to glorify God. Their community, expressed in that locality and made explicit in their worship, was a prophetic but also redemptive act. It was reflecting heaven. Heaven was touching earth. The dynamic of the kingdom was made present. A colony of heaven was being established. The liturgy was priming the pump. At the close they would typically carry on in the Spirit in freedom of worship, in praise and prayer.

I was, however, worrying about myself. This Celtic spirituality had not been part of my personal spiritual background up to that time. I had initially started talking with some excitement to people about what I was reading, but their mystified responses or direct rebukes ("Are you forgetting who you are, where you're coming from? This is not our sort of tradition") stopped me in my tracks.

In late 2000, Daphne and I were invited to join with a number of people who were leaders of movements and denominations across Wales, chaired by the then Archbishop of Wales, the Revd. Dr. Rowan Williams, but convened by a friend of ours, the Revd. Peter Johnson. It was a remarkable time, when the Holy Spirit was clearly present beyond many expectations.

One of the people sharing that day was the Revd. Dr. Martin Robinson, then head of mission and doctrine for the Bible Society. At lunchtime Rowan Williams and Martin Robinson invited Daphne and me to sit with them and talk over the meal. Martin Robinson turned to me after a while and, with that wry air that often characterizes him, asked, "What are the main things that you feel God is opening up for you and leading you into at the moment?"

I hesitated and verbally dallied, but then plunged on, explaining as best I could about my newfound fascination with Celtic monasticism and liturgy, and the mission flowing out from that combination. He looked a little ruffled and accused me of teasing him. Apparently he had just released a book on these very things:

Rediscovering the Celts. I reassured him that my comments didn't have a humorous agenda and bought a copy of the book from him.

I was like a desperately hungry man finding bread. I devoured the book and found it speaking very powerfully to me. The content was great and was all carefully referenced. It opened up another body of literature to me that I was able to read and benefit from. It was wonderful to begin to understand and have a verbal framework that I could use to help describe our infant Celtic-influenced missional community at Ffald-y-Brenin.

Suddenly, here was a model, a descriptive model, that was rooted in history and rooted in our nations. It changed everything. I understood the big picture; I understood what God's broad brushstroke plan was for us. I had clarity about what I was supposed to be blessing, nurturing, and managing.

I was then introduced to the writings of Ian Bradley, who is Professor of Divinity at St. Andrews University. He had written a book called *The Celtic Way*, which described, perhaps slightly romantically, the history of Celtic Christianity in our land. He then wrote a more grounded book called *Colonies of Heaven*, which asked the question "Can God renew Christianity in Britain today through the Celtic monastic model?" I was so challenged by his insights that I presented a copy to each of our trustees, suggesting that our house of prayer thinking was very close to the renewed Celtic monasticism that Bradley described.

He wrote that "we should not forget that the central role of the Celtic monastery was as a house of prayer" (Darton, Longman and Todd, 2000, p. 41). That was at the heart of what was being developed here. He further wrote concerning new "colonies of heaven":

At the very least, these need to have facilities for members of the dispersed monastic/ministerial community to meet and pray together. Ideally, they should be places which can offer hospitality of some form, be developed as educational and resource centres and provide sacred space and sanctuary and the regular rhythm of prayer and worship. (p. 25)

This was a clear representation wonderfully summarizing all that was taking place around us at Ffald-y-Brenin. You can't reflect on this Celtic view of the land and the spiritual history of the local hills and valleys without then focusing on the farmhouse and outbuildings that have become Ffald-y-Brenin.

In the 1970s, a woman named Phyllida Mould had a vision of a place that would be a retreat center. She searched the country but was also quite clear in her own mind that it would not be in Wales. Eventually, not having seen the vision fulfilled, she admitted partial defeat and decided to write the vision down in descriptive form on a piece of cardboard, cut it out in an egg shape, and put it in a Bible. She then informed the Lord that she trusted him to hatch the egg when he was ready.

In 1984, she toured Wales with her husband, Peter, a member of the British Mountaineering Council, who was visiting Wales to chair a meeting. One day, while in Cardigan, he emerged from a realty agent's office and to her annoyance started waving around the sale details of a farm in the nearby hills.

She was unwillingly persuaded to have a look, and they were soon laboring up the steep drive. As they came around the tight bend near the top, she gasped. It was the building she had seen in her vision years before. So they bought it, moved in, and established the Ffald-y-Brenin Trust.

Baroness Cox accepted the invitation to become the first chair, and other notable people joined the committee. Peter gifted much of the land and the buildings to the trust, and some money was raised. A local architect was then commissioned, and Ffald-y-Brenin as we now know it was built, largely with local volunteer labor.

Peter managed the center, assisted by resident wardens to do the day-to-day business. The center was, however, barely viable financially. Peter was the delivery person for the vision, and following his death in 1998, a new visionary leader was needed.

There were clues in their past as to God's future intentions, as I was to discover from the archives several years after I arrived here. A woman from New Zealand, visiting in February 1985 while the place was still being built, wrote:

> I believe that God is saying to Ffald-y-Brenin that it will never move into its destiny until it becomes a house of prayer. He is saying, "I want to open the window of heaven to pour down such a blessing that you will not be able to contain it. It will overflow and pour out in blessing to others. But first this place must become a house of prayer, for through prayer and faith my will can be fulfilled. Dear children, expect great things from me, and you shall receive them."

When she returned in May 1989, she said:

> God has a plan for this place that will not be ful-
> filled until it becomes a house of prayer, but water
> will flow, and healing and salvation and wholeness
> will be poured out through it. He says, "That which
> I have promised I have performed in the past, but
> you have not yet received all that I have for you.
> Do not rest in what you have already achieved, but
> strive to enter into the fullness of the promise. Make
> the vision complete, for the promise still stands. I
> am faithful to my word: my house shall be called a
> house of prayer. It is my purpose that as the water
> flowed from the temple in Jerusalem, so shall living
> water flow from this place, bringing forgiveness,
> healing and peace to heart and mind."

(The water literally began to flow again after we cleansed the
land in a series of symbolic prayer actions.)

Peter and Phyllida did not fully understand what the house of
prayer concept meant, but they got on board with what they had
been told, and a rhythm of prayer was established in the chapel.

God was setting the stage here on the hill of angels. He had
prepared the way for our journey into this new idea of being a colony
of heaven.

We're not building a residential community here at the center,
but we are finding to our surprise that a depth of community is growing up around us; a scattered community is building and forming,

and we're quite happy with that. Our heart is not to draw people to us but to Jesus, enabling people to capture what God is doing here and take it out with them. We want them to be burning with God's passion, wisdom, and fire, having caught the Holy Spirit contagion that is so easily found here at Ffald-y-Brenin.

So far, so good. What was to be the next step on our journey? What was the greater purpose for the flow of blessing we were seeing?

CHAPTER 9

REDEMPTIVE PURPOSE

Some years ago I was running evangelistic breakfast meetings for a few dozen people in the business area of a large UK city. I had invited one particular businessman several times and would also meet with him personally just to chat. One morning, having just eaten breakfast with him, I was back in my office praying when I felt God impress on me that this was the time for this man and not to miss it.

I called him up and asked to see him. He was rather resistant at first but agreed to have coffee ready in ten minutes. His secretary brought in the coffee, and he said to her, "For the next forty-five minutes nobody is to come in here whatever you hear, and I do not wish to be disturbed by the telephone either." She left with a suitable look of concern on her face.

"Peter," I said, "God has told me that this is the time when you have to make a decision. You have been hearing the good news about Jesus. Now God is calling you to acknowledge that you are sinful."

He looked at me and said, "Well, I'm sorry, but I look at my life and I don't see myself as a sinner at all. I do pretty well really. I don't see that there's anything different in my life to the best people I know. I don't think I need a Savior, because I'm not sinful."

"Fair enough. That's no problem, but do you mind if we just pray a moment?" was my response. He grumbled but agreed, so I gently asked the Lord Jesus to cause the Spirit of truth and conviction to come upon my good friend.

There was a moment's silence, then a wail of anguish shook his six-foot-four frame, and he crashed across his desk as he shouted, "God, I'm so sinful. Oh God, I've messed my life up. Oh God, there is so much sin in me. Have mercy."

When he had quieted down a bit, I reminded him of the faithfulness of God and of his promise to forgive. He asked God to have mercy on him, to forgive him his sins because of what Jesus had done, and then he prayed, "Lord Jesus, will you now come and reign in my life and make me a new person, and will you put your Holy Spirit within me so that I can live as a new being in step with you? Come and help me. I'm weak. I'm physically big—as a man I'm exceptionally strong—but at the core of me I acknowledge that I am weak. You are the one who is mighty. Help me. Amen."

He turned to me, wiping the tears from his face, and told me that some years before, he had skidded on black ice and his car had hit a post of some kind. He was knocked out cold but came to as a stranger was dragging him from the burning car. He had been dragged out of certain death into life. He said, "I want to say to you that what you have just done for me is greater than that and I'll never forget it."

A few days later he called me up, saying, "Roy, it's Peter. I've wrecked my life. I've messed it all up. Can you come and talk to me? It's utterly hopeless."

Ten minutes later I was with him. He looked dreadful and asked his secretary to ensure there would be no interruptions. And then a tale of woe unfolded. He felt that he had ruined everything and wasted the good news that he had taken hold of only days before.

I probed gently. He told me that he had had an argument with his wife and had spoken cruel and unhelpful things to her before leaving for work. He had convinced himself that having been forgiven once by God he couldn't seek more of God's mercy or forgiveness.

I sat there and said, "Peter, you really are a hopeless case, aren't you?"

He agreed.

"You really are a sinner, aren't you?"

He indicated that he was and ventured that he was beyond hope. To his surprise I told him that he was only almost right. I picked up my Bible and read to him from 1 John 2:1, which tells us that those who follow Jesus are not to sin, but when we do, Jesus is the advocate who pleads for us.

"I can still be forgiven?" he asked hopefully.

I assured him he could. He jumped up and started praising God. The kingdom of God had truly arrived for Peter.

Salvation had come to this individual when the time was right. What will salvation mean for our communities, and when is the right time to call people away from their sin? If we are to be part of the incoming of the kingdom, what will that mean in concrete terms for our locality?

As the purposes of God continued to unfold at Ffald-y-Brenin, I was starting to wonder afresh about the transformation that can come to people and places as the kingdom comes. We began to find out.

Every week we speak blessings over our neighbors and immediate locality. In Luke 10, we read that Jesus taught the disciples to declare peace over a village or town before entering it. As we developed the practice of blessing our locality, some of the fruits were not just material goods for local farmers. In some cases the coming of the peace of God meant the hold of forces of darkness being broken. This would be more than the failure of local occult practice. Sometimes it was a cessation of criminality.

There is a small National Park car park adjacent to the bottom of our driveway. It was quite notorious, and we were warned not to go there at night because drug dealers would meet there to sort out their supplies and trade with each other. A local farmer once remonstrated with them, and they responded by doing criminal damage to his land.

It was a dangerous place to be, but since we've been praying for blessings, the local farmers tell us that they've stopped seeing the drug dealers come into the area. They came here because it was deserted and a safe place in their eyes to meet and plan and deal. The fact that they don't come anymore is to me part of the redeeming of all things that springs up because of Christ's victory over darkness when he rose again. This is a beautiful area, and we want people to come here and be caught up in the majesty of God's wonderful creation, and through it and through the Spirit of God made manifest, we want them to discover how to know him. We don't want them to feel fearful. The coming of the kingdom destroys the power of fear.

I became aware that I needed to think in a kingdom way about issues that touched the local community. We want to see a healing of relationships between English-speaking and Welsh-speaking people. We want to be a house of prayer where there is healing and reconciliation. For me as a first language English-speaking person, I want it to be clear that I bless, support, stand with, and champion the Welsh-speaking community within Wales. I'm not here to lord it over them or tell them what to do; I want to bless them and support them. It's easy to forget that Wales is a nation with its own history and its own culture that is quite different from the English culture. English has been used as the language of power and domination, and I want to disassociate myself from that. In kingdom terms, we are here as servants.

On a day-to-day basis, however, for most of us the primary concern is how we share the good news with others. How can we tell the story of salvation to those we meet? What is the good news of salvation for the single mother trying to bring up a couple of unruly kids? She can't manage them; she can barely afford to clothe them properly, let alone feed them well. She feels alone in her situation, even as the children become abusive toward her. Perhaps she turns to drink to relieve the pressure. And then the financial woes only get worse.

To walk up to this young woman and say to her "I've got good news for you: you're lost in sin, you're going to die and go to hell, but there's a Savior for you" might be accurate, but in that moment these words are not gospel, good news, at all.

The good news for her, the gospel, is that the God of hope loves her. The God of hope offers to come now, and he can support her, and his people can support her too. She may be facing a tunnel of darkness and hopelessness, but the God of hope can come into her life now and fill her with hope, and he can also transform her children. He's a God who gives; he's a God who longs to be her supplier. We can call on him together, and he'll begin to release the resources to enable her family to have sufficient provisions for the future. This is the gospel; this is the good news for her.

For the homeless man who has nothing and has no future, no hope, no support, walking up to him and saying "I've got wonderful news for you: you're a sinner; Jesus died for you" (unless God has specifically revealed that you should do that) is obviously not the good news he needs to hear.

The kingdom for him is that the people of God care for him and want to lead him into a destiny and the fullness of life that Jesus promised. This may involve helping him find an economic future and a stable place to live. And it seems to me that that's the good news of the gospel for him. When he has absorbed that, which may take minutes, days, weeks, or months, then he will have the ears to hear that he needs to seek forgiveness and be reconciled to God.

We need to understand the wider cosmic struggle that has engulfed the person we seek to share the message of Jesus with. Jesus came to destroy the works of the evil one, and the good news that we impart needs to leave the listeners with the understanding that Jesus can liberate them from the works of the evil one.

That includes political, social, and economic injustice, as well as the powers of addiction and hopelessness. If what we're trying to share or teach or preach to people is not perceived by them to be good news in their situation, then we've probably brought objective truth to them but in an inappropriate way or at the wrong time.

We need to help people see that not only is Jesus our Savior and liberator, bringing us into relationship with God the Father through his death and resurrection, but he is also our pattern and example for life and ministry. He wasn't inviting people to assent to a short forgiveness contract; he was inviting them to participate in a new covenant. They were to be the forerunners of the kingdom.

So what is this good news of the kingdom? The message is actually much more than "You can have your sins forgiven." God has chosen to enter time and space, to destroy the works of the evil one, who had usurped, by man's invitation, the rule of God over the earth. This unfolding of God's purpose on earth involves the created order as well as individuals. His reign has started, and it's here on earth. The kingdom of God has come, it's been activated, all things are being redeemed. This is the good news.

When the Father raised Jesus to life and exalted him to his right hand and gave him all power in heaven and on earth and the name that is above every name, that every knee should bow, it meant that all the existing powers on earth were now called to yield to him (Philippians 2:6–11). When the kingdom of God is released on earth, those other rulers and principalities have to bow, they have to yield; their power is broken.

Jesus did not preach about a kingdom that was way off in the future but one that is in the here and now, in the present. It has drawn near, he said, and it is among us; it has come, and it is amazing news for all who have ears to hear. The fullness is yet to be seen, but right now, where we are, heaven can touch earth.

The disciples were to declare the very same gospel of the kingdom as they went from town to town. He had called them to be with him and to declare the kingdom in power. They were told to bind and loose and to heal the sick as part of their kingdom mandate.

The idea of the kingdom has present significance. It wasn't just a new teaching about what was to come eventually. Jesus says that the kingdom is advancing. It's not simply a vague picture that's been introduced that will make us salivate for the future; it's something that has broken in now and is taking place within creation.

Sin leaves its stain on society, politics, economics, and through many forms of social injustice. The kingdom messenger will want to look at how the works of the evil one are manifest beyond the sphere of our personal rebellion and how the life of the kingdom runs counter to those works.

Sin damages creation. Scripture reminds us that something has cosmically slipped through the incoming of sin. Creation itself is consumed with a groaning that cries out for God to come and restore and reconcile.

> The creation waits in eager expectation for the sons of God to be revealed. For the creation was subjected to frustration, not by its own choice, but by the will of the one who subjected it, in hope that the creation itself will be liberated from its bondage to decay and brought into the glorious freedom of the children of God. (Romans 8:19–21)

> For God was pleased to have all his fullness dwell in him, and through him to reconcile to himself all things, whether things on earth or things in heaven,

by making peace through his blood, shed on the
cross. (Colossians 1:19–20)

We, as the people of God, are caught up in God's redemptive
purpose for creation, for society, for humanity, and for individuals.

We may be tempted toward the passivity that says, "Somehow
we're going to live through life and its difficulties and die with a
groan, but then we're going to be in the presence of the Lord, and
everything will be wonderful." The call of God on our lives is a little
different. We are on the battlefield as part of the force that is concerned with the redeeming of all things. We must see the kingdom of
God break out on earth and all things become subject to him.

The house of prayer will therefore always be a place of words and
deeds done in the name of Jesus as an expression of thankfulness.
Action is merely an act of worship, our prayers made concrete. So we
want a rhythm of prayer that is not just a repetitive use of words but
is engaging with God in power for the release of the kingdom into
this community, nation, and beyond.

A priority for our immediate area is that poverty would flee and
wealth grow. This area has been known as one of the poorest in the
country. We want to see people blessed with plenty as the powers of
poverty are destroyed. It's not that we particularly want everyone to
be wonderfully wealthy (although I see no problem with wealth, only
with the love of it); it's just that we want them to have enough to live
and more besides, so that they can rejoice and become increasingly
generous givers.

A key kingdom value that we hold dear at Ffald-y-Brenin is
that we want to live and act and function with a value system that

embraces mercy, grace, and humility. This in turn will make a difference to the way we interact with people who are living lives that are quite in opposition to the truth of God's Word. We have a choice. Some would condemn these people in the loudest possible terms. With God's help we choose to love them. We want to separate the sinful acts that they may be involved in from the people they have become, believing that with the grace of God and through the Holy Spirit they are invited to become something else.

The Lord's Prayer echoes the Old Testament when it advises us to forgive as we have been forgiven. God advised the people of Israel to look after the orphan and the widow just as he had looked after Israel.

We seek to step into that stance of humility and response. We know that we too have sinned. We choose not to throw stones but to ask God to bring blessing: "Lord, would you release love into these people? Would you release revelation to these people? We bless them. We love them." We desire that God would help us and we would choose to bless others, and we want it to be as natural as breathing. God has not abandoned them. There is hope for them, and we want to pray in the light of that.

We still speak clearly and biblically and state that sin is sin, where it's appropriate, but we do not go up to people who are living sinful lives and start with our analysis of their sin. Jesus didn't. He asked questions, told stories, and invited himself over for meals. His meal interactions spoke acceptance before a word was said to people who were often culturally marginal.

A kingdom worldview says that mercy and grace come first. There were times when Jesus said to people, "Don't sin anymore," but this was often after his release of grace, mercy, and healing. The corrective word came in the warning: don't do that anymore. Let's love; let's pour out grace. This is the lifestyle that I think reflects the kingdom of God.

What might the song of the redemptive community we aspire to be sound like? Perhaps these words go some way toward capturing its essence:

> We welcome all who come here.
> We greet all that we meet.
> May we be as warm and open as Jesus was,
> With a heart for the last, the lost, and the least.
> We don't want to look away
> Or sweep anybody under the carpet.
> With God's help we will not diminish anybody.
> We will be the voices of mercy,
> Blessing all with the love of God
> In the wonderful name of Jesus.

So how do you make this vision a reality in the streets and buildings around you?

CHAPTER 10

LOCAL HOUSES OF PRAYER

As we enjoy watching, experiencing, and blessing the move of God in our midst, we find ourselves overwhelmed with appreciation and love for the ministry of Jesus. Our pattern has been that as we observe and recognize what God is doing, we give thanks and bless it and ask how we might respond to it. He is the potter; we are only clay. He initiates; we obey. We are very reluctant to initiate projects or ministries, because we vastly prefer his ministry to our own.

At one point we began to catch further vision of how God was working with us and how it might be multiplied. In Mark 2, we find that when Jesus entered into Capernaum, people heard that he was in a certain house. That was what we were experiencing. It's what our visitors always say: Jesus is in this place.

Mark went on to describe what happened as a result: "So many gathered that there was no room left, not even outside the door, and he preached the word to them" (v. 2).

That describes life here today. We are often bursting at the seams as people seek Jesus and the word of life.

But there's more. Mark continued with the story of the paralytic who had his sins unexpectedly forgiven and was healed from his sickness. Again, that sort of thing is an ongoing reflection of life at Ffald-y-Brenin.

Our vision was prompted and expanded by the Lord. If Jesus could come and be in our house, why couldn't we share the lessons we had been learning with many others and see a multiplication in our land of Local Houses of Prayer—houses where it is rumored that Jesus is present, with the life-giving word of God, mercy and forgiveness, healing and hope, all being poured out to their neighbors? And if that was possible, why not in offices, factories, schools, hospitals, and so on?

The time had come to give the vision away, but the first time I mentioned it, the result was actually a little comical. I was the guest speaker at a weekend conference in a church on the north Wales coast. On that Saturday morning, I hinted that later in the weekend I wanted to share about the development of what might be called Local Houses of Prayer.

I had barely uttered the words before a well-built man in his early thirties stood up at the back of the hall, stared at me, turned around, walked out, and didn't come back. It was a bit disconcerting to say the least.

Later that day I was having tea at the pastor's home when there was a knock at the door and in came my rather disruptive friend from the morning meeting. He was keen to talk to the pastor and blurted out, "There's something going on in my life that I really need to share with you right now. It's rather urgent."

Despite the fact that we were in the middle of our meal, he was quite insistent, so the pastor offered to talk to him in his study. The man said he was happy to talk in front of me. I was keeping my head down, both literally and metaphorically, but listening intently.

He was off and running now as a torrent of explanation poured out of him. "I was in the meeting this morning and Mr. Godwin mentioned the phrase 'Local Houses of Prayer,' and I suddenly stood up. I don't quite know what happened to me, but it was as if electricity had hit me and I knew this was what I was for. I couldn't wait. I went out of the meeting to go and find my boss, which was hard to do on a Saturday. I found him at home and I gave him my notice, because what I have to do now is develop Local Houses of Prayer."

The afternoon had brought doubt, however. "This afternoon I've been concerned about it, because it's a radical step to take. I have bills to pay. I hadn't shared it with you as my pastor and I need you to tell me whether you think I'm absolutely crazy."

I continued to avoid looking up, but my ears were sharply attuned to the words that came. The pastor gave a deep sigh and then said, "Well, I will have to share it with our eldership, but I'll tell you where I think we'll come from. There is such a sense of God in this that I imagine we'll say that we feel it is right, and we'll stand with you in it. We'll be here to support and bless what you do, so if it turns out to be wrong and doesn't work out, we won't blame you or point the finger. We'll say that we collectively sensed this was right, so we'll collectively stand together in it."

I thought his response was wonderful, and I tried not to audibly breathe a sigh of relief. We discovered one problem, though. Because of his premature departure from the meeting, the enthusiastic young man before us had no idea what a Local House of Prayer might actually be.

Nevertheless within twenty-four hours he'd started a radical house of prayer in an incredibly needy neighborhood, a city sink estate where the local council sought to "bury" needy individuals and families. This was an area with open drug dealing in the streets, high unemployment and crime levels, and children disbarred from every school in the county. He led an initiative to provide toast for kids on Saturday mornings. For many it was the only meal in the week they could be sure of. Fights broke out if the bread ran out. Here was the gospel in action.

Not long after that, I did a teaching series for a pastor. I felt it right that the teaching on the kingdom of God should include an encouragement to create Local Houses of Prayer. What happened over those two evenings was that God touched many hearts and turned people's thinking upside down. Some people who had either been dry in their spiritual lives or felt, for various reasons—sometimes because of their past—that they could never have a part to play in God's purpose, suddenly found that they were being called right into God's purpose. It felt as though the seed of the idea was finding good soil and bearing fruit, and that was wonderful.

So what is a Local House of Prayer? A house where someone prays? Is it just another prayer meeting or house group/cell meeting?

A Local House of Prayer is patterned on the biblical principles we have learned and are experiencing here at Ffald-y-Brenin. It is formed in such a way as to enable the manifest presence of Jesus to inhabit the house, releasing the blessings of the kingdom of God, the rule of Jesus, into an identified area, resulting in salvation, freedom, and deliverance for individuals and transformation of the area itself and glory being given to God.

A Local House of Prayer may be started by an individual, but as soon as possible there should be a minimum of two or three people who have a desire to identify with a particular locality—not a large one, maybe even just a few streets. Fuller detail is shared on our initial training days, which are now held several times a year, but creating a Local House of Prayer demands that we are personally becoming a house of prayer ourselves. Cleanliness is required in our inner being and in the physical house in terms of any sinful or questionable material. Both we and the house need to be holy before the Lord.

Heart attitude needs to be evaluated. We Christians have a strong tendency to criticize and judge people and behaviors we term "sinful." In a Local House of Prayer we are going to change all that and have a heart to love and to bless, to see the good and trust God to deal with the bad. We are going to speak light into darkness and life to the dead, not in judgment but in compassion and love for the sake of Jesus.

As the members meet together in this little colony of heaven, they begin to build an altar to the Lord in the midst of the community with which they are identifying, that praise may arise to the Lord of Hosts. In Ezra 3, we read of the Jews who had returned from exile to rebuild Jerusalem and the temple. They built an altar and started a rhythm of worship there, even though the temple foundations had not been laid.

Building an altar in the Local House of Prayer involves sacrifice, just as it did in Old Testament times. Among our offerings we will bring our worship (not necessarily singing) and the spirit of the community around us. We will need to set aside our rights, judgmental attitudes, pride, and self-righteousness. We will lay down our bodies and our patterns of thinking as living sacrifices for God's glory and his purposes.

We must invoke the manifest presence of Jesus in our midst and know his presence. The next step is to engage in targeted intercession for our area. We encourage prayer that is focused on the release of the kingdom of God so that Jesus is honored in the community and people's lives are set free.

The Lord's Prayer is a great starting point. If we can identify the needs of this micro-community, then we can call on the appropriate name of God and cry out for God to be God in the community. So, for instance, if poverty is a root difficulty, we can call on the Lord, who is our provider, with a prayer such as "Lord, you declared yourself in your Word to be the Lord who provides. Will you come and release provision for these people, that your mighty name might be hallowed in this community?" If we are faced with a community dominated by sickness or hopelessness, we can cry out to the God of hope who is the Lord our healer, and so on.

At the heart of what we seek to encourage in a Local House of Prayer is a willingness to be and to speak blessing into the local community. Think for a moment of the words that are spoken by our society over localities, over families, over individuals: "If you live there you can't be up to much"; "You're never going to become anything"; "Your children are not going to do very well at that school." And think about the seeds of alienation planted by the advertising/consumer complex: "If you don't have this gadget/these shoes and these clothes/that car, you're marginal"; "If you don't look like this, you are second rate."

By contrast, we want to speak blessings and affirmations and mercy. We do this by physically speaking words of blessing over people's lives, circumstances, and communities. For instance, we might say, "I bless every home in the name of Jesus. I bless every wholesome enterprise, that it may be fruitful. I bless the hearts of the people in this community in the name of Jesus, that they may be softened and healed and become increasingly receptive to the voice of God."

Those words will then need to find expression in deeds, and we ask ourselves and each other what we call the Caleb Questions:

1. What is good and wholesome within this community that I/we could bless practically by affirmation and support with time or money? What do I/we see that God has sown into this community that, unbeknown to the people, carries a kingdom value?

2. Who is God putting in front of me/us that I/we should show kindness or mercy to? Is there someone I/we should bless by becoming the neighbor from heaven instead of the infamous "neighbor from hell"? (That does not equate to becoming a well-meaning busybody who is a pain in the neck by the way!) Sensitivity is called for. It might be somebody who's been unwell and is housebound. It might be somebody who doesn't know where to turn next because of personal or family issues. It might be somebody who can't cope with his or her children or his or her garden. In practical ways is there anybody that I/we can show mercy to?

3. Who is God putting in front of me/us that I/we might clearly share the gospel with?

4. Who is God putting in front of me/us that I/we might invite to join with us?

As we answer these questions, we make plans and carry them out. We seek to ask the questions regularly, and there's no pressure in any of it, because it may be that no answers come to mind straight away. That's fine, but we must keep asking the questions. As we begin to engage with the community, the answers will start to become clearer. From the Local House of Prayer comes intercession and blessing, a release of physical expressions of mercy and grace, the words and deeds that affirm, and the blessing and mercy that speaks of the good news of the kingdom.

We want to keep this as simple as possible, because we ourselves are simple people and God has blessed us and done wonderful things because we simply trusted him. To people who say, "Who can actually do this?" I give this clear answer:

"Would you sincerely like to know God more deeply? Would you sincerely like to be able to love people more fully with God's help? If the answer to those questions is yes, then you can do it!"

Over a period of time the aim of the Local House of Prayer is to foster further penetrations of these colonies of heaven into more localities, workplaces, and so on, and this is easily done by releasing members of the Local House of Prayer to go and start another one. Visitors from farther away might be invited to come and experience the Local House of Prayer for a while and then start their own.

Our resources are also available to help local churches to plant a network of Local Houses of Prayer within a geographic area where people can focus together on the needs of that area. It helps people begin to develop leadership skills. So there's pastoral support and oversight already in place, leaving us to bless the leaders and encourage them.

Instead of trying to reshape these groups into tightly controlled units that might reflect the church that's launched them, they can be liberated. They should be thought of as little children: some aren't going to cope too well and are going to have to be brought back in and bottle-fed for a time, but others actually may develop into something totally new that God is doing—a new expression of faith in that locality.

Local Houses of Prayer, offering a rhythm of worship, intercession, blessing, and service, can open people up to join helpful groups such as the Alpha course.

A woman came to see us because she was concerned and discouraged that after having started her Local House of Prayer nine months ago, nothing whatsoever was happening and there was no growth. She'd thought that it would be the means of releasing renewal in her rather barren church, but it was just as dry now.

So Daphne and I sat down with the usual cup of tea and began to ask her questions. As we talked, she began to tell us about the mother who'd run away and abandoned her husband and children; but after they prayed, she came back. She spoke of a woman with severe social difficulties and an inability to talk or interact with other people who had suddenly begun to turn up on her doorstep to talk and interact and find much greater pleasure in life.

As we talked on, we then discovered that this woman had actually started quite a number of other groups in the villages around her, but she'd not joined all this together to see what was going on; she'd missed the fruit. There was a network that was building fresh expressions of the kingdom and releasing blessing into the local community. She was very encouraged indeed once she had connected the dots and recognized what God was doing.

Our desire is to give this vision away. So initially when we started teaching about Local Houses of Prayer and doing training days, I would say at the end to people, "There's nothing here you can join; you can't belong to anything. We've shared the principles with you, and now you must go off and flesh it out and grow it where you are in your situation. It's been good to meet you. Bye bye."

After a while we started getting feedback that although some were doing well, others were struggling and needed support, encouragement, and advice. One day a friend from Sussex, Brian Betts, came into our kitchen, walked up to the draining board, slapped it extremely hard with his hand (which really caught my attention!), and said, "Roy, this is the word of God to you: 'How dare you bring many babies to birth and then place them on the draining board to die!' God says to you, 'Why are you not supporting them and nurturing them and enabling them so that they might live and reproduce?'"

We took his word seriously, and after much prayer and reflection, we decided to create a way of enabling people to link with us and find ongoing support and encouragement. We produced a training package and started an annual conference where people can be encouraged to keep moving forward and have opportunities to share with others who are also leading Local Houses of Prayer.

Caleb looms large for us as a biblical character. He was among those who were called to enter the Promised Land and conquer it. When the people were overwhelmed by the difficulties involved, Caleb challenged them with the words "We should go up and take possession of the land, for we can certainly do it" (Numbers 13:30). His certainty was based on the fact that God had said he was with them.

We want to be like Caleb, having a spirit that is different from those around us, recognizing the difficulties of the present times but choosing to trust in God, who enables us to inherit the promises. We want to follow the Lord our God wholeheartedly and see the kingdom of God released in our land during our lifetime.

As we developed our training resources for Local Houses of Prayer, we began to capture yet more vision. We began to imagine a Local House of Prayer on every street, in every town, on every apartment-building floor, in many workplaces. We began to imagine people being drawn like moths to a light, as they are at Ffald-y-Brenin. We could see the manifest presence of God being released in lives, streets, and offices everywhere—people falling under joy or conviction as they passed the door of a house of prayer. If God could do that with us, he could certainly do it with other houses of prayer.

As the vision grew, I developed a passion for the nations around the Mediterranean and prayerfully began to share it with a few others. Out of that was launched the TransMed Initiative, planting prayer- and worship-based communities all around the Mediterranean, offering a rhythm of prayer, hospitality, mission, and service within each nation.

From the very beginning this has been a partnership with others who come together for the sake of the kingdom and glory of Jesus. In Psalm 2:8, we read, "Ask of me, and I will make the nations your inheritance, the ends of the earth your possession." We are called to play our part in enabling the fulfillment of the Father's promise to his Son.

For us, some key patterns have emerged that are rooted in our values and give shape to our daily ministry. Might these patterns have value for you?

CHAPTER 11

WALKING IN THE ANCIENT FUTURE

From the earliest years of its existence, countless people visiting Ffald-y-Brenin for the first time have asked whether it is a lay monastery. It certainly looks the part as far as the setting, buildings, and grounds are concerned. For most of those years the answer was a chuckle and a clear no. Today the answer might be rather different.

Ffald-y-Brenin was designed and built as a remote retreat center, which it still is. However, it is now so much more besides.

Let me take you on a guided tour.

As you come up the steep driveway from the valley below, the vista opens up. Birds of prey wheel overhead, harassed by the odd seagull. As you round the bend and climb a little more, the buildings come into view. On your left the ground drops away into the valley. On your right it rises toward the ridge from where you look down to the sea and, on a clear day, to the mountains of Snowdonia and the little island of Bardsey, Ynys Enlli, sitting squatly on the horizon.

Walking from the parking lot through the lovely gardens rich in color, the award-winning main stone buildings stretch before you. Accommodation is simple but excellent, with lots of care given to tiny detail, like the carving on the door handles. At the right-hand end is the beehive chapel, well known for the mountain bedrock that emerges in the middle. Suddenly appearing from its hiding place behind the chapel is the Hermitage, a fairy-tale building with a vaulted ceiling, galleried bedroom, bubbling stream, and beautiful views.

At the opposite end of the buildings the courtyard contains the meeting rooms, with their spectacular views across the valley below to the hillside opposite. Your ears pick up the muffled cries of intercession arising from the prayer room as we pass.

Walk through the courtyard to the back of the main buildings and you will see a long rockery, with heathers giving color for most of the year and a waterfall feeding the pool that nestles below. The old farmhouse fronts the lawn.

Carry on through the avenue of trees to the stunning views from the promontory, and pause at the significance of the high cross standing before you. Breathe in the presence of God. You are on holy ground. This is a "thin" place, where heaven is easily accessible. Prayer is easy. Feel the hush. Healing hangs in the air.

Explore the grounds, carefully tended by Rob over a number of years. It is so easy to find quiet space. Wander onto the open hillside and find streams, waterfalls, woods, and wildlife in abundance. Walk for miles if you are energetic enough.

If you have arrived on your own, you will be self-catering during your stay here, but if you are part of a group and have asked us to feed you, you are in for a treat. Early on in our time here we took steps to develop the ministry of hospitality. This had always been a self-catering center, but we wanted to offer a catering option for groups. The way it turned out was typical of God's workings here.

I was in Evesham to meet Peter Middlemiss, the man who had prompted me to find out more about retreat centers. As we chatted, he dropped in a very strange sentence—at least to my ears. He said, word for word, "I believe that the philosophy of the food and the way it's presented must accurately represent the philosophy of the ministry of the house." The conversation carried on, and eventually I set off for home. But that sentence wouldn't leave me as I traveled. What on earth did he mean?

I think God deliberately put a veil over my mind. I couldn't understand what it meant, but it wouldn't leave me alone. When I repeated the sentence to Daphne, she couldn't work it out either. So we prayed about it. A week later somebody mentioned to us the name of a local woman who was renowned for her cookery skills, and we soon discovered that she went to a local church. Daphne and I hatched a plot and invited her to come to Ffald-y-Brenin and have coffee with us.

We wanted one of those "let's find out what she is like" chats. She agreed to come, but at the appointed time there was no sign of her. Our hope was faltering. Reliability is fundamental when you have a flow of guests. Daphne and I had a coffee together, and I was leaving to go to the office when I saw a movement and looked across the lawn, and there was the woman, standing by a wall, looking down over the valley, unmoving.

I came back, mentioned it to Daphne, then carried on. A quarter of an hour after that, we heard a knock at the door and there she stood, saying, "I'm so dreadfully sorry to be late; it's not like me at all. I was here on time. I've not been here before and I simply found myself rooted to the spot, and there's something I want to ask you."

She then came straight to the point and asked us whether we really only wanted to give her a cup of coffee or whether we were checking her out as a potential cook. This completely undid our strategy. I hadn't wanted to be in a semiformal interview conversation, so I just looked at her and asked why she was asking.

Her response was astonishing. She told us, "I stood looking over the valley thinking, my goodness, if I was invited to come and cater here, I would want to let go of all my European catering, international catering, cuisine nouveau, because I would simply want to see that the philosophy of the food I produced and the way it's presented matched perfectly with the philosophy of the ministry of the house."

There was a momentary lull while our chins fell on the table. I just looked at her and prompted her to explain more. She told us that she felt the food that should be offered to guests here should be simple but excellent farmhouse country fare. Well produced, well presented with love.

That was it. We asked Marilyn to start as soon as possible. She's still with us some years later, an incredible treasure, and along with her helper, Brenda, unleashing welcome blessings on our guests and fighting off marriage proposals from men who have tasted her bread and butter pudding!

HOUSE OF PRAYER

At the heart of our life here is the daily rhythm of prayer, liturgically framed so that all may join in, whatever their background, without feeling ignorant or marginalized. Morning and evening we honor Jesus as Lord and bring the sacrifice of praise. Our midday meeting (actually at 12:45 p.m.) has been a particular blessing, as it slows us down and allows us to realign ourselves with the Holy Spirit after the pressures of the morning have done their best to take our eyes off the Lord. Night Prayer often leads in to exceptionally restorative sleep. Guests are not obliged to join in the rhythm but are welcome if they choose to.

Various prayer meetings continue throughout each month, and our monthly Prayer Day is enjoying the breath of life as prayers are answered, lives are touched, and testimonies of healing and joy are given. We can no longer accommodate the growing numbers on-site and are grateful to the local chapel in the valley below for making their hall available to us.

Many guests come here to pray and seek the Lord, and for most it is the place of breakthrough. Visions are seen, dreams arise, the whisper of the Almighty is in their ears and in their hearts, and praise and thanksgiving erupt.

Networks of prayer are rising up as we commit ourselves to intercede for the nations. The Caleb Prayer has become an international phenomenon. We are involved in national and international prayer movements as we cry out to God for mercy on our own land and for workers to be raised up and thrust out. Daphne is passionate about all issues related to Wales and the beautiful Welsh language, and she leads prayer meetings in Welsh.

Local Houses of Prayer are being planted in increasing numbers, and significant prayer-based mission initiatives are being launched.

SANCTUARY

Ffald-y-Brenin offers sanctuary, a refuge, for many people over the course of a year. This is a prayer-soaked, presence-filled place where it is safe for the troubled to find rest. God does not disappoint us. Many are the stories of grace.

When Philip, a church leader, arrived, it was with the sole purpose of spending four days fasting and praying to break through and hear God's direction over a very complicated situation. Several hours after his arrival he asked apologetically whether we would be too offended if he left straight away. Concern probably showed on our faces, to be replaced with silly grins as he explained that God had already spoken to him. He was clear minded and needed to leave and put things right with those he had hurt and offended. Such stories thrill us.

A NEW MONASTICISM

A number of years ago I felt a cry rising up in my inmost being—"There has to be more than this." As I remembered my dreams of what living as a child of God would be like, there was that cry again. There has to be more than this. I was stirred by memories of great days in the past when God had seemed so close, but that's where they were—in the past. Oh God, there must be more than this.

Looking at church initiated the same cry. There is so much good, so many signs of blessing in many local churches and fellowships, but looking more broadly at the national scene raised the question "Is this really all that the Father has in mind for the bride of his Son?"

These cries reflect the searching of the early desert fathers. And I sensed that this was more than merely the cry of my own heart. I could hear echoes of it in the conversations I had with others as they reflected on their own lives and the reality of church life. I believe that God himself has put that cry in people's hearts because he's stirring them up.

Our experience of God in recent years has been profoundly enriched by what we call renewal. But we've outstayed our camping permit because the fire has died down and the cloud has lifted, and it's time to break camp and move on. It's a new day. There are new shapes, new experiences, and new depths to explore out of the fullness of God's riches. We are not leaving renewal behind. We carry it with us on the journey.

Such times of moving are unsettling. When we find ourselves on the edge of a new thing, we can be unsure as to which direction we should take. For us, we have set out on a journey of discovery within what we call a new monasticism.

Dietrich Bonhoeffer, the German church leader who provoked the Nazis by resisting them and the rest of the church by writing about the cost of discipleship, wrote in one of his wise letters that it was about time people formed a new monasticism by banding together and living by the principles of the Sermon on the Mount.

It is his phrase, "a new monasticism," that enables us to explain the work of God that is going on in our hearts and lives at Ffald-y-Brenin. Rowan Williams, the current Archbishop of Canterbury, has commented that whenever the church has failed to live up to the expectations of the people, a new form of monasticism has always arisen. Such forms have usually led to the renewing of the church.

The story of early monasticism is the story of mission. When Saint Martin established a monastery in Tours, he used models from the desert to guide him but was very clear that mission was to be at the heart. Evangelistic teams were regularly sent out into the countryside to bring the good news of the inbreaking kingdom to the poor. When Saint Ninian visited Martin, he caught the vision and built a missional community, Candida Casa, in the Galloway region of Scotland.

Others used the same model: vibrant, inclusive fellowship based around a rhythm of prayer and worship, reality in discipleship, and powerful witness and mission. Their communities lived according to a common rule of life that enriched their lives.

Any new monasticism must be outward looking. When people talk of prayer, they sometimes say that we need to retreat in order to advance. Jesus would take time alone before pivotal events that would shape the destiny of himself, his disciples, and the people to whom he ministered. And so it must be for us. We're not turning our backs on the world; we're drawing strength from God so we can engage with the world in a way that reflects the life and message of Jesus.

What we long to see is the kingdom of God breaking in, areas being liberated spiritually, people responding with joy, the harvest of the kingdom being seen. So to enter this new monasticism is not to retreat from the world; it's actually to engage further with heaven so that we can engage further with earth.

When we look at the call of the disciples, we find Jesus calling them to be with him and to go out to proclaim the kingdom, heal the sick, and release the oppressed (Mark 3:14; Luke 10:1–9). If everything in our lives flows out from his presence, then we will see the words, works, and wonders come from the overflow of his work in us. Instead of seeking to make things happen, we won't be able to stop them when we speak truth about Jesus. So often we have quoted Zechariah 4:6—"'Not by might nor by power, but by my Spirit,' says the LORD Almighty"—and then exerted all our might, power, and manipulative methods to make something happen. Now is the time for God to be God.

At the end of the Narnia tales C. S. Lewis coined the phrase "further up and deeper in." We want to do just that, and in fact to go "deeper in and further out." We want to press deeper into God, but for the sake of the gospel and for the sake of Jesus, we want to press further into the world too. We want to carry his presence and the power of the age to come with us so that the kingdom breaks in now for people and for localities.

Simplicity and childlikeness are at the heart of how we seek to live. We trust God and take him at his word, firmly believing that all his promises are "Yes and Amen" in Christ. Our hearts' desire is to know him more, engaging our hearts, imagination, and bodies.

Opening up historic monastic spiritual practices dating back to the desert fathers and mothers of the third century has given us fresh perspective. Here we have found helpful tools that are enriching our spiritual lives, engaging every part of our beings in prayer and communion.

As the Spirit of God has blown across us, we have found increasing numbers of people asking how they might connect with us. I have been very slow to respond to such requests. It would seem wrong for anyone to follow me or Ffald-y-Brenin. We want to stay hidden and let Jesus be the only one on center stage. But when increasing numbers found themselves saying that this was home as soon as they arrived, we had to listen to God for clearer direction.

As we began to share our underlying values and vision with others, they seemed even more determined to connect with us. And so an international network of radical kingdom seekers called the Caleb Community is emerging, a scattered connection of people who share with us in exploring a new way of living and of mission, rooted in the anointing of the Lord and in historic Christian precedents.

For the Revd. Sister Barnabas it has been an unlikely journey. I had returned from a mission trip and was driving to the coast with Daphne for a breath of sea air when she dropped a bombshell. I was as stunned as she had been as she explained that a well-respected Baptist minister in South Wales and long-term visitor to Ffald-y-Brenin, the Revd. Valerie Davies, had called to say that she was going to become an Anglican nun.

We were lost for words and laughed in disbelief. God has a good sense of humor; unexpectedly he spoke and said that we were connected with this. We had no idea what that meant but received the odd excited phone call to tell us how it was all going. Eventually she called to say that she wasn't to be an Anglican nun but a praying sister connected with us. It didn't seem very likely, but a few months later the General Secretary of the Baptist Union of Wales joined with me on a baking hot September evening to induct Valerie Davies as a full-time prayer-based Caleb explorer, as Sister Barnabas, or "Bee" as she is now known.

Others' stories are generally less spectacular but no less significant.

EVENTS AND CONFERENCES

Visitors are not always residential. We welcome thousands of non-residential visitors each year.

Guests are welcome whenever we have room to welcome them. Our main purpose is to create the sacred space where it is easy to encounter God. We hold events throughout the year that aim to feed into and enrich the lives of those who connect with us.

Many churches bring their own people and leaders to do their own thing here in the context that is Ffald-y-Brenin. It is an exciting place for Alpha Holy Spirit days because of the ease with which he flows here.

Sometimes it's hard to put a label on Ffald-y-Brenin. Here are some of the terms that have, quite rightly, been applied to it:

Retreat
Sanctuary
Hospitality
House of Prayer
Resource Center

A growing, scattered connection of explorers
Workers going to the nations
Blessings being experienced and spoken out
Churches encouraged
The favor of the Lord of Hosts is upon us

Like Caleb, we have been spying out the land that the Lord our God is giving us. It looks exciting and daunting at the same time. We have passed the spying stage and have now crossed the river, accompanied by a growing band of explorers. We are living in the land and tasting of its goodness, but there is much ground yet to be taken. We are walking in an ancient future.

Now we long to raise an army of Jesus-hungry warriors to join us and carry God's mission forward; not armed with swords but armed with a hunger for adventure and a longing to see sinners forgiven, the oppressed delivered, the sick healed, prisoners released, the naked clothed, the hungry fed, the poor rejoicing, those in prison visited, the church renewed, and Jesus glorified.

We pray for hundreds of ordinary people to connect with us in the journey and conquer the land as they establish Local Houses of Prayer. We need gifted witnesses and personal evangelists who can relate to the people we meet on the way. We need able teachers who can speak and demonstrate the life of the Spirit. Not experts. Learners like us. To hold the word of God in their hands and set apart Jesus Christ as Lord in their hearts.

The kingdom of God is near. Welcome to the monastery. Would you like to explore with us? If this has stirred you, please let us know. This is the place where Jesus opens the door.

AFTERWORD

The story you've been reading so far is not my story; it's the story of the Father's heart. Maybe you have found yourself thinking at times, *I wish my life had been as straightforward, clean, and tidy, and I could be the kind of person God uses to do these sorts of things.*

Well, I have news for you. The story of my life has not been clean and tidy and nice; in fact, it's been extremely messy. If anybody deserved God's blessing, mercy, and grace, it wouldn't be me. But God's story is always the story of taking the weak, the wounded, the helpless, the despised, the rejected, the little things, and the remote things and displaying his glory.

That is the story of this book: the unfolding of the Father's heart toward us. It's his story and it's his glory that we seek. If God can act like this with me, who knows what he could do with you?

So I want to ask you whether you have heard the call of Jesus to simply be with him. The first question that this provokes is "Do you really know him?" As you've read the stories in this book and seen God's unfolding work, have you found a little voice within you saying, "I don't really know how to relate to God like this"?

If that's where you are, then I want to tell you that there's good news: It's not about being good; it's about being forgiven. It's not about being strong; it's about being weak so his strength can come into you and be displayed within your weakness. It's not about your perfection; it's about his perfection. It's not about your life having been perfect and pleasing to God; it's about the life of Jesus having been pleasing and perfect for God and now available to come and live within you, changing you from the inside out.

If you would really like to know him, the starting place is honesty. Find a quiet place and say, preferably aloud:

Father, I acknowledge the reality of who I am. I acknowledge the weakness, the sin, the mess in my life and I ask you to come and have mercy on me, just as I am, because of who Jesus is.

So with your help I take my sin, my weakness, my pain, my grief and place it all on the cross where Jesus died, so that he can carry it away and then forget it forever. I let go of these things now.

With your help I choose to let go of grudges and bitterness, and forgive all who have wounded me.

Father, would you please put the Spirit of Jesus deeply within me and begin to shape me and refine me? Will you begin to do what I cannot do? Will you begin to produce within me the person you've always wanted

*me to be? Will you please begin to lead me in the paths
you've always planned for me? I ask this in Jesus' name.
Amen.*

It may be that as you've read this book and seen the stories
unfold, it's reminded you of how you used to know God and how
you used to relate to him. It may be that you are able to remember
times in the past when God really blessed you.

Although you are now talking of our Lord Jesus Christ and
speaking clear words, the truth is that you're no longer heart-to-heart
with him. You're not hearing the Holy Spirit whispering the Father's
secrets into your heart.

If that's you, now is the time to do something about it. There's
the good biblical word *repent*, which simply means "turn around;
make a decision." For you the prayer declaration will be "I'm going
in a different direction now. I'm going to make a fresh start. From
this moment on I want to seek the heart of God, I want to burrow
into the promises of God, I want to be so close to him that I hear his
heartbeat and catch his passion for me and for others."

It might be that you're desperate because you've got yourself
caught up in busyness, and the pressure of life has crowded out time
and made it almost impossible to find space to be quiet, to be still,
to listen to the Father's voice, and to read his Word. If that's where
you are, then perhaps you need to ask, "Am I living the life and the
lifestyle that God has called me to? Am I in the right place?"

If your answer to those questions is yes, then you need to begin
to find ways of building in some space, and it may be minutes in a
day, or half an hour in the week, but within the pressure of life you're

going to have to find space to be still, just to know him and to hear him.

Perhaps you are aware of a great cry arising within you:

"My Christian life is not what I thought it was going to be. I'm so frustrated and disappointed, because I thought there was going to be so much more than this."

If you feel that cry welling up within you, I want to suggest to you that the Father himself has put it there. Because that's what he's doing at the moment with his people. If that's your cry, you are echoing the cry of the Holy Spirit who teaches us to pray even when we don't know what to say.

The good news is that there really is a lot more than this. The Father is calling us back to simplicity, back to trust, back to childlikeness, back to the exercise of his power instead of our power. It really is not by our might or strength but by his Spirit. There is a new start available, a new depth, and a new life.

The next thing I want to ask you is whether you have engaged with Jesus' commission for the sake of the kingdom and for the sake of the lost. Have you actually engaged with his purposes in the situation where you are, in the confines of where you live or work, and within your lifestyle choices? Have you engaged with his redemptive purpose so that you personally are an agent for the kingdom of God where you are? If that is so, you need to be engaging with people. It's insufficient to engage with his purpose without engaging with the people around you. He has sent his Spirit to help us. While we look for methods, he sends his Spirit.

Paul speaks in his letters of those who are coworkers for the kingdom of God. I want to invite you to become a coworker for the kingdom of God. This same God who's taken what is weak, what is hopeless, what is sinful, what is at the ends of the earth and displayed his mighty power is your God too. His heart for you is the same as it is for me.

So will you engage and become a coworker for his kingdom? Why not gather one or two others with you and begin a Local House of Prayer? Why not share with one or two others whose heart cry is "More, Lord" and together cry out to God for an empowering for simplicity and a deeper Christian life?

I remind you again of the call of Jesus to his disciples, first of all to be with him and secondly to be agents of the kingdom, and in Jesus' name I invite you back into that which is the heart of the good news of the kingdom.

And finally (as I'm sure you've heard many a preacher say) I invite you to connect with us if you would like to find resources, to join with others in sharing what they're finding, and to share testimonies of what God is doing.